LEONID <ins>Petrovich</ins> GROSSMAN

BALZAC
AND
DOSTOEVSKY

translated by
Lena Karpov

ardis

Copyright ©1973 by Ardis

ISBN 0-88233-038-1 cloth
ISBN 0-88233-039-X paper

Table of Contents

BALZAC
AND
DOSTOEVSKY

Dostoevsky's first printed work was his translation of *Eugénie Grandet.* This was the preface to his entire literary career. Not *Poor Folk,* which did not appear in print until two years later, but the first Russian translation of Balzac's celebrated novel is the narrow gate into the creative world of Dostoevsky.

In many respects his artistic proximity to Balzac was not accidental. The author of the *Human Comedy* held a central place among the European writers who impressed the youthful Dostoevsky and left a permanent mark on his writing. It would seem that none of his other early teachers touched on so many crucial questions of his own conscience or so keenly dealt with all of the riddles of life which concerned him most.

Balzac turned out to be the writer closest and dearest to the young Dostoevsky. He brought new pleasures to the burgeoning imagination of the nervous seventeen-year-old dreamer and cleared new and unknown roads in the realm of creativity. For Dostoevsky, Balzac long remained, as Virgil for Dante, *lo maestro e l'autore*—a teacher who let him share the secrets of his art, and a faithful guide through all of his dark and dangerous journeys. With all the fervor of untempered genius, Dostoevsky threw himself into the febrile world of the Balzac novel, and even to the end he would not forget his first impressions from reading the *Human Comedy.*

In many respects it accompanied him everywhere. The unknown author of the still unwritten *Poor Folk* initiates his literary career under the sign of Balzac with the translation of *Eugénie Grandet;* almost forty years later, in a work written just before his death, the "Pushkin Speech," he cites

Balzac and Dostoevsky

Balzac to confirm the main thesis of his later philosophy.

The history of Dostoevsky's acquaintance with Balzac goes back to his first period of intensive reading—the middle of the 1830s. At that time, according to A. M. Dostoevsky, the issues of the review *Library for Reading* appeared in their home and became the exclusive property of the two older brothers. This is unquestionably the first source of Dostoevsky's acquaintance with the young French novelist, who had not yet achieved world fame. And though Senkovsky's journal had an extremely suspicious attitude toward the youthful French literature of the thirties—it made ironic remarks with identical prejudice at the expense of Hugo, George Sand and Balzac—it was forced to submit to the authority of their growing fame, and even to place translations of their novels in its pages.

In the first issues of 1835 the *Library for Reading* prints a translation of *Père Goriot* directly from the pages of the *Revue de Paris,* but with a few abridgements. Here Dostoevsky could also find a sympathetic critical evaluation of the two Balzac novels which were destined to remain central in his work—*Eugénie Grandet* and *Père Goriot.* These first critical studies of Balzac which the young Dostoevsky chanced to see are of the greatest interest for the history of his literary development.

According to the review in the French journal, Balzac's talent had developed markedly in his last two novels, *Eugénie Grandet* and *Père Goriot.* At last, remarks the reviewer, Balzac had found what he had so long been searching for—a truly unhappy woman. According to the journal, the French novelist had created a poor, emaciated, green, hysterical world for himself, a sick female society, a huge hospital for chronic diseases of the female heart.

Jules Janin's comments on Balzac are cited in one of the succeeding issues of the *Library for*

Balzac and Dostoevsky

Reading. Describing the milieu and background in *Père Goriot* the French critic notes: "It was an amusing mixture of everything in the world—opinions, vexations, sympathies, pity, despair, ignorance, learning, and poverty reigned over all of this disgusting chaos. The motto of the house was indigence and loneliness. The house in which they live on nothing but bread is characterized by an absence of all family ties; a house such as this is something in between a prison and a retreat for beggars; here one can constantly be certain of everything—of hunger, of being cold, of sickness, and of health; here money is collected bit by bit, just as the rag-man on the street counts on the rags which are thrown out of houses. Balzac found an excellent introduction to this world."

Thus, in Balzac's very early period he was presented to the Russian reader not only as an interesting story-teller with a "quick and productive mind," but also as a depictor of all the dark sides of life—poverty, sickness, loneliness. The atmosphere of his works was defined just by the comparison to the jail, hospital and retreat for beggars.

It is not surprising that given such intensive interest in the personality and works of the French novelist, Dostoevsky uses the summer vacation of 1838 to read "almost all of Balzac," who, incidentally, had by no means finished his career at that time.[1] It was at this time that Dostoevsky exclaimed, "Balzac is great! His characters are the creations of a universal mind. Such a development in the soul of a man was prepared not by the spirit of the time, but by thousands of years with all of their turmoil."

From this comment alone, which is quite exceptional in its ecstatic quality, it is clear what a deep impression this reading made on Dostoevsky and what an ineffaceable mark it was bound to leave in his memory.

And in fact, seven years later his delight was

just as intense. According to Grigorovich, a comrade and intimate witness of the first steps of Dostoevsky's literary career, Balzac remained his favorite writer even up until his graduation from the Central Engineering School. "I have translated *Eugénie Grandet*— a marvel! a marvel!" he writes to his brother at this time. He is literally delirious about this Balzac story. "I am finishing a novel the size of *Eugénie Grandet*," he says by way of definition of his own first work. Even the laurels received by Balzac's heroes give him no peace. When, in this same period, he has to compose a comic advertisement for Nikolai Nekrasov's satirical almanac, he is inspired by the first feuilleton of Balzac's Lucien: "My advertisement is causing a lot of talk," he informs his brother, "because it is the first time there has been such lightness of touch and such humor in a piece like this. It reminded me of Lucien de Rubempré's first feuilleton. My advertisement has already been reprinted in the miscellaneous news in *Notes of the Fatherland*."

The reference to the French hero is extremely characteristic of Dostoevsky's literary interests during this period. He apparently has in mind the first steps of Lucien in his career as a Parisian journalist, described in the second part of *Lost Illusions*.

Lucien had read one of those interesting articles which made the fame of the small paper, in which, in two columns, one described some of the little details of Parisian life—an image, a type, an everyday event, or some sort of strange occurrence. This model of the feuilleton, entitled "Parisian Passers-by," was written in that new and original manner where the idea is born from the clash of words, where the resonance of epithets and modifiers awakens the reader's attention. (H. Balzac, *Oeuvres complètes*, Ed. Houssiaut, Paris, 1955, VIII, 296.)

Such is Balzac's characterization of a model of humor and new style, one which Dostoevsky attempts to follow in his first try at a magazine feuilleton—the literary genre in which he subsequently tested his own strength. Balzac's influence is felt even in the language of Dostoevsky's letters from this period. They are studded with the favorite words and expressions from all of the jargons in the *Human Comedy,* as Dostoevsky himself notes. "The military academy—*c'est du sublime,"* he exclaims in one of his letters to his brother, copying the style of Balzac's poets and actors. "The undertaking . . . has been *irrevocablement* begun by us," he writes in another letter, reproducing the language of Balzac's businessmen. "Chernoglazov—*un homme qui ne pense à rien,"* he defines someone using the same style. "We will think about Revel, *nous verrons cela* (old Goriot's expression)," he notes himself in one of his subsequent letters. And for a long time after this Dostoevsky recalls one of the most characteristic expressions from *Père Goriot,* perhaps under the immediate refreshing of his impressions by his re-reading of Balzac in the sixties. This is Vautrin's expression *"assez causé,"* which Dostoevsky introduces into his polemical articles and even into his novels—in *Crime and Punishment* it is cited by Svidrigailov.

Thus in the period when he read most eagerly, during the reading which he remembered best, Dostoevsky read all of Balzac from his first period, read him to the point of imitation, to the point where he needed to share Balzac's work by translating it, even to the point of adopting the terminology and style of his literary idol.

II

Now the question arises—how do we explain the fact that after having read Balzac in the first year of his arrival at the Central Engineering School in 1838, Dostoevsky shows a special interest in him during the mid-forties? Did something happen in the meantime which rekindled his interest in the French novelist?

Balzac and Dostoevsky

What happened was Balzac's arrival in St. Petersburg in 1843. The great interest in his work, which was definitely felt in Russia at the very beginning of the thirties, reaches the proportions of an outright literary fad at the beginning of the forties, placing him in the center of the Russian reading public's attention and firmly establishing his fame as the greatest literary force in Europe.

At this time the pages of Russian journals are filled with Balzac's name and the titles of his works. In the periodical press there is a re-examination of statements made earlier about the French novelist—ones which were not always favorable to him—and there is a serious effort to pronounce some final word about his novels. Among Russian journals the groundwork was laid for that critical tendency which in subsequent years would be expressed when Balzac was declared a rare expert in matters of the human heart, an inimitable analyst of passions, a magician and sorcerer of words, one of the most remarkable men of his time, and one of the premier writers of his epoch.[2] This laudatory, at times even ecstatic, evaluation of Balzac in Russian criticism of the forties could not go by unnoticed by Dostoevsky.

Balzac spent three months in Petersburg in 1843, and he was in the center of the capital's attention the whole time. The *Northern Bee* never stops returning to this main topic of the Petersburg day.

"First of all we will share with our readers news which is interesting to all lovers of literature," the newspaper reports apropos of his arrival, "The famous French writer Balzac arrived on the steamer Devonshire which landed from London and Dunkirk last Saturday, the seventeenth. It is said that he intends to spend the entire winter here . . ."

A few days later the paper prints a long essay on the recent French novel, dedicated mostly to Balzac. The author of the essay has a critical attitude toward many of the "European celebrity's" works, but his whole essay bears witness to the wide popularity of Balzac in Russian society during this period. The analysis begins with the words, *"Une ténébreuse affaire* is of course already well known to our readers . . ."* and it ends with a veritable hymn of praise to Balzac: "With all our soul we confess that we consider him one of the best novelists of our age. *Eugénie Grandet, Histoire des Treize,* and many other novels have won the author laurels which will never fade . . . "

In one of the following issues the paper cites the "favorite expression of Balzac" with a prefatory note of praise. Finally, the writer's departure is noted: "Today, Saturday, the celebrated Balzac, as we have been informed, is leaving Petersburg." Pointing out the malicious epigrams of the French press about Balzac's journey to Russia, the newspaper concludes, "Balzac will always remain one of the foremost writers of his age . . ."[3]

This whole reevaluation occurs precisely at the time when the twenty-year-old Dostoevsky, having finished his education, begins intensive preparation for his literary debut; and totally absorbed in his numerous creative, translation and editorial projects, he follows current Russian journalism with increased attention.

Balzac's popularity among the literary youth of this period attains vast dimensions. D. V. Grigorovich, Dostoevsky's closest friend and one-time roommate, describes how he first stepped across Belinsky's threshold with great emotion, having thought over in advance exactly the words he would use to express his love for Balzac to the celebrated critic. But Belinsky's unexpected attack on the author of *Eugénie Grandet* immediately disillusioned Grigorovich about the critical authority of the creator of the *Literary Reveries.*

Grigorovich was also present at one scene of public expression to Balzac of the feelings of Russian readers for him. It happened in one of the Petersburg theaters. Scarcely had Balzac appeared in the loge than his name rushed through the crowd. Young people surrounded him with loud expressions of delight. The French critic Champfleury subsequently described this event from the words of Grigorovich himself,[4] from whom Dostoevsky too no doubt immediately heard about the triumph of the author of *Eugénie Grandet* in the Russian theater.

This event should have strongly intensified Dostoevsky's interest in Balzac, which even so was already deep. It undoubtedly lent to his abstract literary attraction to Balzac a more intimate character and strengthened his feeling for the writer whose personal appearance in Petersburg had aroused such delight among Dostoevsky's closest friends.

Thus at the very dawn of Dostoevsky's literary activity in 1843, when he was just humbly beginning his translation of *Eugénie Grandet,* Russian criticism provided a thoughtful, serious and deeply sympathetic evaluation of the author of that literary "marvel." And because of his arrival in Petersburg at that time, Balzac stood at the center of public attention and completely won over the sympathies of Petersburg's literary youth.

This general uproar around Balzac's name probably prompted Dostoevsky to begin immediately the translation of that tale which had not yet appeared in Russian. In the spring of 1843 he began to translate *Eugénie Grandet.*[5]

III

The history of Dostoevsky's relations to Balzac is not exhausted by the period of the forties. In Dostoevsky's later, post-imprisonment period he shows the same exceptional liking for the literary idol of his youth.

In this respect the critical department of his journals *Time* and *The Epoch,* which is full of references to Balzac, is of great interest. Striving in his journals to restore cetain unjustly repudiated or forgotten spiritual values, Dostoevsky puts the author of *Eugénie Grandet* in the fore along with the creator of *Don Carlos.* In one of the very first issues of his journal *Time,* in an anonymous note on Schiller, Dostoevsky intercedes for poets and novelists of the West who have been underrated by Russian critics, and Balzac is put first.

"Many poets and novelists of the West appear before the court of our critics in a kind of ambiguous light. Not to mention Schiller, for example, let us recall Balzac, Victor Hugo, Frédéric Soulié, Sue and many others about whom our critics, beginning in the forties, have written with extreme condescension. To some extent Belinsky too is guilty before them. They did not suit our overly "realistic" criticism of that time" ("Something on Schiller," *Time,* II, 1861). In this remark of Dostoevsky we perhaps hear an echo of personal insult for his tale *The Double* being underrated by Russia's "overly 'realistic' criticism." In any event, it is characteristic that Dostoevsky places Balzac's name at the forefront of the unforgivable omissions of which Belinsky is accused.

In his journals Dostoevsky apparently strives to correct this error of the critics in the forties.

Soon after the note we have cited, he prints an article by Apollon Grigoriev containing references to Balzac in the criticism department. Given the unquestionable influence which this remarkable Russian critic had on Dostoevsky's thinking, these scattered literary characterizations are of special interest.

Characterizing the new French literature of the thirties, Apollon Grigoriev remarks that it is impossible "not to believe that the great analyst of the human heart, Balzac, is right in asserting the true existence of the eccentric *Human Comedy,* lurid and diverse pictures of which he revealed more and more in each of his works."

Balzac and Dostoevsky

With his remarkable insight into the essence of
Balzac's originality, Grigoriev asserts that the Russian
Natural School of the forties "had to bow down to"
Balzac. "There was perhaps no writer in France more
real than he. And he stands totally alone in all litera-
ture in the character types he created. Recall *Old
Goriot, Eugènie Grandet, The Poor Parents*—and all
of his great works."

And the next year, speaking of the new, painfully provocative poetry of the large cities, Grigoriev
makes a remarkable juxtaposition of Gogol, Balzac,
Nekrasov and Dostoevsky. All four of them seem to
him creators of a poisonous fantasy of the modern
capitals. He characterizes Petersburg of the middle
of the century as a special city which unites intellectual and moral philistinism with the exceptionally
cerebral development of the Russian character.

"Recall even Gogol's *Nevsky Avenue* and you
will understand what I am trying to say. The great
depictor of the 'banality of the banal person,' without knowing it himself, took the depiction of banality
to the point of something grandiose, almost equalling
the attitude of the great author of the *Human Comedy* to his Paris. Recall also the first works of the poet
of *The Insulted and the Injured,* especially *The
Double,* that painful and terrifyingly exhausting
study of events not of life, but of pure mirage . . ."

In all his ecstatic comments on Balzac *Time's*
critic is undoubtedly in solidarity with its editor.
Another issue of *Time* that same year contained an
abridged translation of William Raymond's public
lectures on French literature, in which Balzac is
given special attention. He is declared the "most
powerful" of all the realistic novelists, and the *Human Comedy* is called an unfinished, "gigantic, all-
embracing work." In the words of this critic, Balzac
"enjoyed a great vogue in France, particularly after
his death." The new generation considered him a
"great analyst of the human heart, a great philosopher."

Balzac and Dostoevsky

Such are the comments on Balzac in Dostoevsky's first journal. Obliquely, but definitely, they testify that Dostoevsky's early esteem was unchanged. And as a matter of fact, in the middle of the sixties Dostoevsky reread Balzac again. This is what Anna Grigorievna Dostoevsky told me about this in a personal conversation: "When we got married and went abroad, Fyodor Mikhailovich undertook, as he put it, my 'literary education.' The first book he gave me was *Père Goriot*, then came *The Poor Parents.* We reread these novels together in French. His favorite writers were always Balzac, Walter Scott, Dickens and George Sand."

The length of this attachment is amazing. Because thirty years after his first acquaintance with Balzac, after living through the scaffold, imprisonment, forced service in the army, the banning of his journals, the celebrated writer, growing old now, drops into a Russian reading room in quiet Florence to read the latest issues of newspapers received from his homeland, and quite accidentally he finds a collection of Balzac's novels. And in spite of the urgent work, the material need, the debts, the eternally calling pages of the unfinished *Idiot,* the eternally troubling questions of editorship, Dostoevsky, nearly sixty years old, again rereads, as he had at seventeen, these absorbing pages. And in certain isolated touches in his later novels one again feels the emotion with which the graying Dostoevsky reread his first teacher after such an eventful life. Rogozhin's house in the *Idiot* echoes the description of the dwelling of the old Grandet, and Stavrogin shares Dostoevsky's special interest in Balzac's female characters.

And during this same period, in the *Diary of a Writer,* Dostoevsky declares that as early as the thirties Balzac had produced works such as *Eugénie Grandet* and *Père Goriot,* to which Belinsky was so unjust, because Belinsky totally overlooked their significance in French literature.[6]

Balzac and Dostoevsky

In the seventies Dostoevsky's library contained a complete collection of Balzac's works in the original, and the novel *César Birotteau* in a separate edition.

And, finally, one of Dostoevsky's most important references to Balzac occurs in the manuscript of his speech on Pushkin. Among the numerous corrections and deletions, this passage remains untouched in the manuscript text. We cite it here directly from the manuscript of the "Pushkin Speech" which is held in the Public Library in Petrograd.

After these words: "Would you agree to be the architect of such a building with this condition? And could you even for a minute accept the idea that the people for whom you are erecting this building would themselves agree to accept their happiness if, let's suppose, it were founded on the suffering of an insignificant creature, a mercilessly and unjustly tortured human being, and that having accepted this happiness they would remain happy forever?"—after these words, which occur, with minor variations, in the printed texts as well, in the manuscript this undeleted passage follows:

In one of Balzac's novels a certain young man, depressed over a moral problem which he is not strong enough to resolve, addresses a question to one of his comrades, a student, asking him: "Listen, imagine that you don't have a penny, and suddenly, somewhere far away, in China, there is a decrepit sick mandarin, and all you have to do here in Paris, without moving, is to say to yourself, die, mandarin, and he will die, but because of the mandarin's death some sorcerer will immediately bring you a million and no one will find this out; and the main thing is that he is somewhere in China, and he's a mandarin no matter whether on the moon or on Venus—well, would you want to say, die, mandarin, so that you could immediately get the million?" The student replies: *"Est-il bien vieux ton mandarin? Eh bien non, je ne veux pas!"* That is the French student's decision. Tell me, could Tatyana decide otherwise than the poor student, Tatyana with her elevated soul, with her profoundly suffering heart? No, and the Russian soul decides the same way: all right, let me be deprived of happiness, but I don't want to be happy while dooming someone else. This is a tragedy, it has happened and it is impossible to go beyond this barrier; it's already too late, so Tatyana sends Onegin away. (Manuscript of the "Pushkin Speech," Petrograd Public Library, page 5.)

This passage is extremely important. It shows us first of all how long Dostoevsky's youthful attraction to Balzac lasted. He is the only European writer who delighted Dostoevsky in his schoolboy letters and to whom he turns for philosophical argumentation in his last work. If the translation of *Eugénie Grandet* is the threshold to Dostoevsky's creative world, Balzac's thought in the "Pushkin Speech" serves as a kind of support-beam to the cupola into whose form Dostoevsky's later philosophy was so permanently cast. It is remarkable that he turns specifically to Balzac to reinforce one of the basic tenets of his philosophy, central not only to the "Pushkin Speech" but also to *Crime and Punishment* and *The Brothers Karamazov*—the impossibility of building one's happiness as an individual or even the general good on the suffering of another person, even if it be an insignificant creature. This application of Balzac to his own ideas on the tears of the tortured child, this application of a passage from *Père Goriot* to Dostoevsky's famous page on Tatyana's act of moral heroism, is the best proof of the vast importance Balzac continued to have for the late Dostoevsky.

Such is the history of Dostoevsky's literary acquaintance and kinship with Balzac. Dostoevsky loved Balzac, valued him highly, and was keenly interested in him throughout his lifetime. Of course, this could not but leave an imprint on his own works.

IV

Let us turn to Dostoevsky's printed works. The

Balzac and Dostoevsky

translation of *Eugénie Grandet* is a most interesting introduction to his work. Apart from the chance reasons which led him to undertake this work, one essential and central factor was functioning here: attraction to a similar genius. With the very first books of Balzac, whom according to Grigorovich Dostoevsky considered "far superior to all other French writers," he felt that inner kinship between the French novelist and his own still maturing gift, the kind of thing which immediately turns a fortuitously discovered writer into a teacher and model. For Dostoevsky, Balzac turned out to be the kind of fortuitous literary discovery which gives a decisive creative impulse to one's first immature and inchoate ideas. In Balzac's novels Dostoevsky found not only the plots and character types of which he was still vaguely dreaming for his own works, but at times even whole sentences which flashed through his consciousness already written down before him by a foreign writer.

Certain pages of *Eugénie Grandet* provided direct suggestions to Dostoevsky for isolated ideas and details in his own later descriptions. Such, for example, is the description of Prokharchin's treasure, modelled on Balzac's description of Eugénie Grandet's purse.

First she sorted out twenty Portuguese moidores struck in 1725 in the reign of John V. Then five genovines worth one hundred livres each in Genoa, exchange value of each eighty-seven francs. Then three Spanish gold quadruples of the time of Philip V, minted in 1729. Then, and this most pleased old Grandet (because it was twenty-three carat gold in every coin) one hundred Dutch gold pieces minted in 1756 and each worth twelve francs.

A collection of medals and *rare coins* precious for numismatists and misers: three rupees with the sign of the Scales and five rupees with the sign of the Virgin, whole, pure gold, twenty-four carats each, each of them worth thirty-seven francs, forty centimes. Finally, a *double Napoleon* which she had received the day before yesterday

from her father . . . This treasure consisted of coins which
were clean, shiny, polished; old Grandet often admired them
and would discuss their beauty for hours with his daughter;
he explained their rarity, the clarity of the minting, the shine
of the edges, the elegance of letters still fresh, shining and
unworn by time.

(Repertoire et Panthéon, 1844, tome 7, p. 62, italics
mine.)*

Noble one-ruble coins, solid seventy-five kopek coins,
a good fifty-kopek coin, the plebian twenty-five kopek
coins, twenty-kopek pieces, even the old-cronish petty cash
which promised little, five and ten-kopek silvers—all in special
paper containers, in the strictest and most methodical order.
There were rarities too: two metal bits of some sort, *one
double Napoleon,* one unidentified but obviously *very rare
coin . . .* A few of the ruble pieces were also from very ancient times; worn and nicked Elizabethan German crosses;
Petrine coins, the coins from Catherine the Great's time for
example were now very rare, old fifteen-kopek coins pierced
for wearing as earrings, all absolutely worn down, but with
precise demoninational markings; there was even copper, but
all of it already green, rusty. They found one red paper note,
but there was nothing more.

(Dostoevsky's Works, I, 311, italics mine)

Here Dostoevsky transformed Balzac's description into the Russian monetary system, preserving all of the basic features of Balzac's picture. "The
rare coin" is mentioned in both descriptions, and in
both cases money which has already gone out of
circulation is described—in both places the mintings
from the eighteenth century, the times of John V
and Philip V in Balzac, the epoch of Peter, Elizabeth
and Catherine in Dostoevsky. Finally, particularly

---

*Grossman fails to note that Dostoevsky translated
less than one half of the description as found in Balzac and
mixed up several numbers. In general his translation of the
novel is extremely inaccurate. *(Translator's note.)*

25

Balzac and Dostoevsky

worthy of note in Dostoevsky's description is the gold double Napoleon in a pile of five- and ten-kopek pieces—it fell into Mr. Prokharchin's mattress directly out of Eugénie Grandet's purse.

Several other descriptions from Balzac's novel can be felt in the pages of Dostoevsky's later novels too. For example, it is interesting to compare the description of Rogozhin's house in the *Idiot* with the first page of *Eugénie Grandet:*

Occasionally in the provinces one finds houses in appearance gloomy and melancholy, like ancient monasteries, like wild, sad ruins, like dry, sterile, naked walls . . . This kind of gloomy, melancholy appearance, it would seem, was the characteristic feature of one house in the city of Saumur.
("Repertoire et Panthéon," 1844, book 6, p. 386.)

One house, probably because of its peculiar *physiognomy,* even from a distance, had begun to attract his attention. This house was large, gloomy, three-storied, without any architecture, a dirty-green color . . . Both from the outside and inside somehow inhospitable and dry, all as if hiding and concealing something, but it would have been difficult to explain why it seemed so just from the physiognomy of the house. Of course, architectural outlines have their own secret.
(Dostoevsky's Works, VI, 207, my italics.)

In the original there is an expression which Dostoevsky changed in his translation, but which he subsequently recalled: *physionomie d'un logis.*

Dostoevsky's translation is quite free. In places it even turns into a retelling. The translation avoids the temptations of literalism everywhere. In the very first sentence he expands Balzac's description with supplementary epithets. He expands the text of the original in almost all of the descriptions:

Il se trouve dans certaines provinces des maisons dont la vue inspire une mélancholie égale à celle que provoquent les cloîtres les plus sombres, les landes les plus ternes ou les ruines les plus tristes.

Balzac and Dostoevsky

Occasionally in the provinces one finds houses in appearance gloomy and *melancholy,* like ancient monasteries, like *wild,* sad ruins, like *dry,* sterile, *naked* walls. . .

The superlative degree of the original is replaced by an abundance of new epithets in the translation.

But it is far from everywhere that Dostoevsky succeeded in conveying precisely the energetic style of the original. It is worth comparing the following passages:

Le regard d'un homme accoutumé à tirer de ses capi-taux un intérêt énorme contracte nécessairement, comme celui du voluptueux, du joueur ou du courtisan certaines habitudes indéfinissables, des mouvements furtifs, avides, mystérieux, qui n'échappent point à ses coreligionnaires. Ce langage secret forme en quelque sorte la franc maçonnerie des passions.

The glance of a man accustomed to looking at gold, taking pleasure in it, shines with a sort of vague secret expression, grasps hidden nuances, acquires inexplicable habits, like the glance of a voluptuary, a gambler or a courtier; this glance is quick and timid, greedy, secretive; others in this position know it, they have learned it: it is the accepted sign, the secret Masonic sign of the passions.

Often Dostoevsky avoided the difficulties of exact translation and shifted to a free re-telling:

Financièrement parlant monsieur Grandet tenait du tigre et du boa; il savait se coucher, se blottir, envisager longtemps sa proie, sauter dessus; puis il ouvrait la gueule de sa bourse, y engloutissait une charge d'écus et se couchait tranquillement, comme le serpent qui digère, impassible, froid, méthodique.

In business he was adroit, *greedy, strong* as a tiger, as a boa. He knew how to hide his claws if the situation demanded, to crouch, to await the moment and finally leap at his victim. Then he would stretch open the *awful* maw of his purse, pour the gold pieces into it, pull the string, hide the purse—and all of this with self-satisfaction, coldly, methodically.

This translation served as Dostoevsky's literary school, which in many ways formulated his own manner as a writer. Pondering with pen in hand every sentence of the celebrated French novel led the literary novice deeply into Balzac's technique of narration and revealed a whole series of creative secrets which he did not know. In this sense, the translation of *Eugénie Grandet* is reflected in Dostoevsky's writings to the end.

But above all Balzac's novels helped in his ideological development. It somehow intensified the evangelical tendency of his work which, even in periods of the strongest skepticism and misanthropy, constantly directed him to the themes of "poor folk," to the humble and the rejected. This is one of the main reasons for Dostoevsky's attraction to the author of *The Poor Parents.* Balzac was among the writers who with their artistic preaching of compassion helped him to resolve once and for all the problem of Christian art which always interested him.

This little book, despite the eighty Balzac novels which appeared subsequently, is still Balzac's most unquestionable right to immortality; it is one of the most important depictions of everyday suffering in nineteenth-century literature, suffering devoid of tragic effects, without any preaching, and depiction of profound compassion for the silent victims of life. The evangelical tendency which Balzac constantly strove to introduce into his novels, stories, and novellas attains its greatest depth, purity and transparency in his story of a "humble person" silently crushed by the wheel of fate.

This subtle tragedy had to grip Dostoevsky immediately. The author of *Eugénie Grandet* plays a noteworthy role in that profound creative emotion which Dostoevsky always experienced when dealing with the theme of the insulted and the injured. His story of innocent outcasts and submissive sufferers long remained in Dostoevsky's memory as a great marvel of sincere understanding, as the highest of creative achievements.

The pitiful fate of a woman is the main theme of Balzac's story. The main meaning of Balzac's *chef d'oeuvre* is in the image of the silent and humble Eugénie, in her uncomplaining anticipation of happiness (which does not come) and in her meek acceptance of innumerable disillusionments.

Truely, with the figure of this tragic virgin he brilliantly solved that most difficult task which Dostoevsky subsequently faced with indecision: the creation of a positively beautiful figure not tainted by any comic features.

For Dostoevsky, Balzac's story always remained the model for the psychology of a meek woman. From "The Little Hero" and *Netochka Nezvanova* to "A Meek Woman" and *A Raw Youth,* he never ceased being inspired by this female character from the *Human Comedy,* whom in his youth he dreamed of as a living creature.

"This woman reminds us of an angel because suffering creatures belong to her . . . She was one of those women who are born to be martyrs." "To feel, to deeply love and almost always suffer with their love—this is the fate and destiny of woman." (F. M. Dostoevsky's translation of *Eugénie Grandet,* "Repertoire et Panthéon," 1844, VII, 80.)

Dostoevsky apparently recalled these passages from the novel often. "There are women," he writes in one of his early stories, "who are like sisters of mercy in life. When talking to them one does not have to hide anything—at least, nothing that makes the soul feel pain and hurt. He who is suffering goes to them boldly and hopefully without fear of being in an uncomfortable situation; but then it is a rare person among us who knows how much infinitely patient love, compassion and absolute forgiveness some female hearts contain. Whole treasures of sympathy, consolation and hope are held in these pure hearts, which are so often hurt—although their wounds are carefully concealed from curious eyes, because profound grief is most often silent and secret. They are frightened neither by the depth of a person's wound, nor its infection, nor its stink: whoever goes to them is worthy of them, and they seem born for great deeds . . . "

This is how the Eugénie Grandet figure is characterized in Dostoevsky's works. The quiet and sad Alexandra Mikhailovna in *Netochka Nezvanova* and Madame M. in "The Little Hero" roughly outline the later development of the same type in the figures of Sonia Marmeladova, the quiet angel Sofia Ivanovna, or the irresponsible Grushenka in *The Brothers Karamazov*.

Other works of Balzac, particularly his *Père Goriot,* strengthened the evangelical or philanthropic trend of Dostoevsky's work in the same direction. *Père Goriot* contains a stunning contrast of the inclination of human nature to cruelty, for greed for power and pleasure—with its capacity for unlimited self-sacrifice. Not in vain did Balzac himself call the novel a monstrously sad creation which produced the same impression as a disgusting wound.

The novel's main hero is a pitiful and forgotten old man despised by everyone. In his pension in the Latin quarter, father Goriot serves as much a living butt for derision and mockery as Mr. Prokharchin in his quarters. Among the regulars of a run-down pension in Balzac's narration is one pitiful creature destined for mockery and humiliation.

"How did this contempt mixed with hate, this persecution strike the eldest of the pensioners himself? Perhaps it is characteristic of human nature to force a person to bear this who can bear it like a martyr, out of true humility, weakness or indifference. Don't we all love to show our strength at the expense of others?.. If the human heart is often delayed on its road to compassion, it rarely stops on the precipitous slope of hate."

And striving to emphasize this evangelical tendency in his novel, Balzac says of his hero: "To depict the face of this Christ of fatherly love one would have to find comparisons among the images created by the greatest artists to show the passions lived through by the Savior of humanity for the happiness of the world."

Here of course there is no need to speak of Balzac's direct influence on Dostoevsky. The reasons for the eternal struggle of the creator of Zosima to resolve the problem of Christian art are so deeply embedded in his own personality that to study them one must turn to the primary source—the spiritual character of Dostoevsky himself. Balzac (or Hugo, Dickens or George Sand) can only give direction to already inherent creative strivings and provide examples of this religious element in artistic creation. And in this respect direction was definitely given. With his books about the outcast and the insulted, Balzac provided Dostoevsky with remarkable models of how a realistic story can be permeated by evangelical undercurrents, and Balzac showed Dostoevsky the truest paths to the resolution of the problem of Christian creativity in the art of the modern novel.

V

1866 is one of the most important dates in the history of modern European literature. The year when *Crime and Punishment* was published. This novel, which is one of the highest achievements in a series of creations by Dostoevsky, should attract special attention from the scholar: it is the first work of Dostoevsky in which he managed to express himself broadly, freely and completely, putting into his idea all the painful experience of the trial he had lived through, but preserving, as he did so, the kind of beginner's freshness and infectious joy typical of his early works. One feels that a liberated genius, long constrained and crushed by circumstances has finally, for the first time, spread its wings to their full gigantic width, freely soaring to the height appointed it, and exulting in the scope and boldness of its flight. This sense of youthful boldness and fervid creative enthusiasm was never again repeated in Dostoevsky with such purity. In the novels which follow one often feels a certain weariness, the intensity of creative pitch is not identical everywhere; and nowhere do we again find the ringing intensity of Raskolnikov's drama all through a single work.

But, like almost all great creations of verbal art, this Dostoevsky novel has its roots in earlier literature. *Crime and Punishment* marks the apogee of Balzac's influence on Dostoevsky. It is unthinkable to study the basic idea of the novel and a number of the peculiarities of its development without turning to Balzac. To do this one has to look into that current in the *Human Comedy* which runs counter to its evangelical tendency, trying to overwhelm and control it. The themes of liberated individual will, of a mighty and dominating spirit which stands on the borderline of morality and has the right to transgress all generally accepted prohibitions—the problem of the superman—attracted Balzac no less than the problem of Christian art. This is where his kinship to Dostoevsky is reflected most strongly.

The passage from the manuscript of the "Pushkin Speech" which we cited above already indicates to us a certain closeness of Raskolnikov to Balzac's ideas. According to Dostoevsky's version, in one of Balzac's novels a "poor student" depressed over a

moral problem which he is not strong enough to resolve puts to his comrade the question about the
right to kill a useless creature, asking it in the form
of a parable about a decrepit, sick mandarin. The dilemma is posed with extraordinary sharpness and
definition: "Well, would you want to say, die, mandarin, so that you could immediately get the million?"
The Parisian student's question outlines the moral
problem which the poor Petersburg student, Raskolnikov, strove to resolve in his melancholy de-
pression.

The passage which Dostoevsky cites is from
Père Goriot. This novel is an essential prolegomenon
for the study of *Crime and Punishment.* The history
of Eugène Rastignac is one stage in the formation of
the superman who is taking his final tempering in
crime. One of the main ideas of Balzac's novel is the
right of the higher man *(l'homme supérieur)* to step
through blood to attain his elevated and beautiful
goal.

Circumstances force the poor student, who feels
in himself the possibility and demand to raise himself
from his state of humiliating poverty to summits
where a strong personality leads a free existence, to
face a tormenting dilemma: he has only to allow a
crime, to become a passive and unresponsible accomplice to a murder and he will become the possessor
of an estate of many millions, i.e., fulfill all that his
greedy egoism demands. He struggles for a long time,
refusing to give his consent to the murder, but when
the crime is committed without his permission, after
a new series of inner conflicts, he accepts the conse-
quences which are profitable to him because of the
evil deed which has been committed, and he therefore
achieves his goal by stepping through blood. —Such
is Rastignac's story in *Père Goriot.*

Let us follow the phases of this fascinating
psychological drama. In the beginning of the novel
Rastignac is in great need: he is crushed by the

involuntary comparison of his grandiose plans with pitiful and disgusting reality. He begins to understand the power of money; he decides irrevocably, "I will get it" and assumes the words of a woman close to him as his motto: "Be an executioner."

But the main thing is that he decides to achieve his goal quickly and immediately. As soon as the decision is made, Rastignac receives letters from his mother and sister. These pages, which testify to the willingness of people close to him to sacrifice themselves for him, strengthen the decision he has made. "Oh, yes!" Rastignac exclaims, after reading the letters, "Money no matter what! I would like to give them as much happiness as possible."

And now, when life has already set the task of rapid acquisition of power before him, the systematic development of superhuman power begins in him. His chance neighbor in the pension, the escaped convict Vautrin, outlines his seductive doctrine to him. With the first words of their discussion Vautrin declares to Rastignac:

". . . you should know that killing a man means as little as that!" and he spat. "But I make a point of killing him decently, and only when it's absolutely necessary. I am what you might call an artist. I have read the *Memoirs* of Benvenuto Cellini, and in Italian too! He was a rare sportsman, and he taught me to follow the example set by Providence who kills us right and left haphazard, and also to love beauty wherever it is to be found. Isn't it a fine game to play, after all, to be alone against mankind and to have luck on your side? I have thought a great deal about the present constitution of your social disorder. . . . There are only two courses to follow: stupid obedience or revolt. I obey in nothing, is that clear? Do you know how much you'll need in the direction you are going? A million and at once; without it we might as well go and cool our hot little head in the drag-nets at Saint-Cloud to find out if there's a God."

He sketches for Rastignac a picture of ordinary,

traditional human activity, and he concludes:

"Oh, it would be better to become a pirate than to dirty
your soul this way . . . It would be better for you to begin
your revolt against all human conventions right today . . .
The crossroads of life is before you, young man, choose.
But then you've already chosen."

"Fifty thousand young men at this very moment are in
your position and are racking their brains to find a quick
road to success. There are as many of you as that. You may
judge of the efforts you must make and the bitterness of
the struggle. You must devour each other like spiders in a
pot, seeing there are not fifty thousand good positions for
you. Do you know how a man makes his way here? By
the brilliance of genius or the cunning use of corruption.
You must cut a path through this mass of men like a
cannon-ball, or creep among them like a pestilence. Honesty
is of no avail. Men give way before the power of genius,
they hate it and try to blow upon it because it takes without sharing the plunder, but they give way if it persists; in
short, they worship it on their knees when they have
failed in their efforts to bury it under the mud . . . .
Draw your own conclusions . . . .
You, if you're above the common herd, go straight
forward with your head high. But you will have to
fight against envy, slander, mediocrity, against the whole
world. Napoleon came up against a Minister of War called
Aubry who just failed to send him to the Colonies. Sound
yourself! See if you will be able to get up every morning
with a will more determined than it was the night before . . .
Remember that the superior man uses events and cirum-
stances to control them."

And Vautrin proposes a sure way for Rastignac
to achieve power. In their pension lives a girl who is
in love with Rastignac; her father is a multimillionaire
(Taillefer) who has disinherited her, giving it all to
his son; it is him that Vautrin undertakes to kill in
a duel, thus shifting the whole estate of the old
millionaire to Rastignac's future fiancee. The student
has only to agree to the convict's plan and the murder

of the young Taillefer will raise him to the pinnacle of power.

Rastignac firmly refuses, but a mute struggle begins within him which will cease only when he becomes the unwilling accomplice of Vautrin.

Vautrin's plan does not leave Rastignac's mind for a moment after this. He constantly ponders the pro and contra of the problem set before him; he is often inclined to decide, persuading himself that "I must become a cannon-ball as Vautrin says" and his thoughts revolve unceasingly around this tormentingly irresolvable problem. Rastignac wanders through the streets of Paris, in Dostoevsky's words, "depressed over a moral problem which he is not strong enough to resolve." It is during one of these walks that the conversation between the two students took place, a conversation which Dostoevsky remembered so well that in the first draft of the "Pushkin Speech" he cited it from memory with almost literal accuracy, even using a French quotation.

Afterwards he spent nearly the whole day idly loafing, a prey to the fever in the brain well known to young men afflicted with too lively expectations. Vautrin's arguments gave him food for thought, and he was lost in meditation upon the social order when he chanced to meet his friend Bianchon in the Jardin du Luxembourg.

"Where did you get that solemn face?" said the medical student, putting an arm through his, and walking on with him towards the Palais.

"Temptations give me no peace."

"What kind of temptations? Temptations can be got rid of."

"How?"

"By yielding to them."

"You may laugh, but you don't know what you're laughing at. Have you read Rousseau?"

"Yes."

"Do you remember the passage where he asks the reader

what he would do if he could make a fortune by killing an old mandarin in China by simply exerting his will, without stirring from Paris?"

"Yes."

"Well?"

"Bah! I'm at my thirty-third mandarin."

"Don't play the fool. Look here, if it were proved to you that the thing was possible and you only needed to nod your head, would you do it?"

"Is your mandarin well-stricken in years? But, bless you, young or old, paralytic or healthy, upon my word—The devil take it! Well, no."

"You're a good chap, Bianchon. But suppose you loved a woman madly enough to turn your conscience inside out for her, and she needed money, a lot of money, for her clothes, her carriage, all her whims in fact?"

"You turn my head, and then ask me to use it!"

"Oh! Bianchon, I'm out of my mind, see if you can cure me. I have two sisters who are angels of beauty and innocence, and I want them to be happy. Where am I to get two hundred thousand francs for their dowry within five years? That's the question that confronts me. There are circumstances in life, you see, when you have to play for big stakes and it's no use wasting your luck picking up pennies."

"But you're simply stating the problem that every-body entering on life is faced with, and you want to cut the Gordian knot with a sword! If you act like that, my dear fellow, *you must be Alexander, otherwise you go to prison.* I'm quite content, myself, with my humble fortune . . . . Even *Napoleon* could only dine once, and could have no more mistresses than a medical student takes . . . I come to the conclusion that the Chinaman should be allowed to live." (My italics, L.G.)

But Rastignac is no longer as categorical as Bianchon. The circles of his steady march toward solidarity with Vautrin narrow every day. Even his friend notices this.

"So, we've killed the mandarin?" Bianchon asked him one day getting up from the table.

Balzac and Dostoevsky

"Not yet," answered Rastignac, "but he's at his last gasp [*mais il râle*]!"

The medical student took the answer as a joke, but Rastignac was not joking.

Meanwhile Vautrin is continuing his work.

"I startled you at first when I gave you a glimpse of the mechanism of the social machine, and put you up to the ropes, but your first fright will pass off like a conscript's on the battlefield, you will get used to regarding men as soldiers who have made up their minds to die, in the service of those who are crowned kings by their own hands . . . . But now I propose to help you to a handsome fortune at a nod from you which compromises you not at all, and you shilly-shally . . . ."

". . . I live in a sphere raised above that of other men. I consider actions as means to an end, and the end is all I see. What is a man's life to me? Not that!" and he snapped his thumbnail against his teeth. "A man is everything to me, or nothing at all. He is less than nothing if he is a Poiret: you can crush him like a bug, he is flat and smelly. But a man is a god when he is like you; he is no longer a piece of mechanism covered with skin, but a theater where the finest sentiments find play . . . . I wouldn't talk like this to everyone, but you're not like an ordinary man, I can tell you everything because you can understand it."

In the final version of *Père Goriot* which we have Rastignac remains indecisive until the end. But the first version of Balzac's novel ended in a totally different way, the version printed in translation in the *Library for Reading* in 1835, the version which also came out in the thirties in separate Russian editions, the version known to Dostoevsky from his reading of all of Balzac in 1838. In this first version Rastignac crosses the rubicon.

He looked at this humming beehive as if he wanted to suck all of the honey out of it, and he uttered this fateful exclamation:

"Now you and I will divide this up!"

Balzac and Dostoevsky

He went to Paris. On the road he still wavered between heading for the beautiful house on Rue d'Artois or his former dirty lodgings at Madame Vauquer's, and he found himself at the doors of the house of M. Taillefer: Vautrin's shadow led him to this house and put his hand on the handle. He squinted his eyes so as not to see it. He was still searching in his heart and in his poverty for an honest excuse. Victorine loved her father so tenderly! Rastignac asked for Mme. Coutoure. Now he was a millionarie and as proud as a baron.

(*Library for Reading,* III, 1835, "Foreign Literature," 106.)

In other words the mandarin has been killed, and the poor student attains the power he desires with the help of his millions.

VII

For all the differences in the character and fate of Rastignac and Raskolnikov, their ideological kinship is indubitable. The problem which they strive to resolve is the same: the right of the superman to transgress, and use crime to achieve his highest destinies. Rastignac's parable of the decrepit mandarin millionaire corresponds to Raskolnikov's "principle" about the old woman usurer. The conversation between Parisian students which so struck Dostoevsky is repeated almost word for word in *Crime and Punishment:*

"Come now, I want to put a serious question to you," said the student hotly . . . "On one hand a stupid, senseless, insignificant, evil, sick old hag, unnecessary to anyone, and on the contrary, harmful to everyone, who doesn't know herself what she is living for and who might die tomorrow by herself . . . On the other hand young fresh strength perishing uselessly without support, and thousands of cases like him, everywhere . . . "

"Of course, she is unworthy of living," observed the officer, "but that is nature."

39

Balzac and Dostoevsky

"Well, my friend, nature has to be directed and corrected, or else we would drown in prejudices. If it weren't for this there would not have been a single great man . . . Wait, I'll ask you another question. Listen to this!"

"No, you wait, I'll pose a question for you."

"Well?"

"So you rant and rave like this now, but tell me—would you kill the hag yourself or not?"

"Of course not. For justice I . . ."

(My italics. L.G.)

This, of course, is a paraphrase of Balzac's conversation about the mandarin, with the same concluding answer. Thus the main idea is expounded in both novels.

Let us trace the maturation and development of this problem in the souls of the main victims—Rastignac and Raskolnikov.

The roads which their spiritual tragedies follow correspond. In the beginning of the novel Raskolnikov, like Rastignac, is given tormenting alternatives: serious poverty, the prospect of getting out of it by the usual way and with long work, or on the other hand, the possibility of getting all of the capital at once in order to immediately display his superior gifts. Raskolnikov, apropos, is a law student like Rastignac, caught up in the same life dilemma: he stands, in Balzac's expression, "between need and studying the lawcode" *(entre le code et la misère)*. But the prospect of intensifying his need does not attract him. Rastignac needs, as Vautrin puts it, "a million and quickly," almost word for word Dostoevsky's formula. Raskolnikov is frustrated by the task of slowly pushing along the roads of life.

"They pay children in coppers, what can you make out of kopeks?"

"And you need all of the capital at once!"

"Yes, all of the capital," he replied firmly after a moment of silence. "If it's five kopeks at a time, what can I do?"

Balzac and Dostoevsky

Let us recall Rastignac: "There are times in life when one has to play big and not waste one's happiness on earning pennies."

While Raskolnikov is facing this problem, which has come to confront him directly, he gets a letter from his mother. This is a device from Balzac's novel. At the analogical moment Rastignac gets a letter from his mother and sisters. For all the difference of the letters in the two novels, the letter's importance in the further strengthening of both heroes in the resolution which has been outlined is identical. What we might call the *sister motif* is introduced into the psychology of both students, by means of this picture of humble self-sacrifice by those near and dear. There arises a personal dilemma intensifying the essence of the general dilemma—which has already grown to the proportions of a real moral problem: how will poverty affect the sisters' futures? What destructive experiment will life perform on these innocent and beautiful girls if they do not have the essential material resources? "Angels of beauty and goodness," says Rastignac of his sisters. "Dunya is an angel! Dunya is a creature as noble as an angel!" Raskolnikov's mother says repeatedly in her letter. Rastignac does not go as far as Raskolnikov's ruminations on the "percent" which threatens his sister, but the psychological effect of the letters received is identical: poverty will be reflected destructively not only on the candidate for hero-dom himself, but also on those who are near and dear to him. The problem of personal will is complicated by the altruistic motif and made into a profound moral problem.

But the motif of testing one's superhumanity through crime remains dominant: "If you're above the common herd, go straight forward with your head high," as Vautrin puts the tormenting problem to Rastignac. "Man is god when he is like you," he says, approving of him to shed blood. The names of Napoleon and Alexander are cited by the convict and the student friend in Balzac: "You want to cut the Gordian knot with a sword," says Bianchon to Rastignac, "if you act like that . . . you must be Alexander, otherwise you go to prison." These are variants of the question which never ceases to burn at Raskolnikov: "Am I a trembling worm, or do I have the right?" The images of Napoleon and Alexander the Great serve to inspire and guide him too.

Raskolnikov does not consider the usurer a human being. In the tavern he overhears a student say something which he remembers: "What does the life of this consumptive, stupid and evil hag mean on the general scale of life? No more than the life of a flea, a cockroach, not even that . . ." As we have already seen this is almost what Balzac wrote word for word. "What is a man's life to me?" asks Vautrin. "He is less than nothing if he is a Poiret: you can crush him like a bug, he is flat and smelly."

Dostoevsky also outlines the main situation of Raskolnikov's inner drama using Balzac's scheme of things. Rastignac's psychological conflict is sharpened by the combination of two influences. On the one hand the whole horror of life opens up before him, the whole painfully confused mass of cruelties, humiliations and heroic self-sacrifices. Such is the story of old Goriot, agonizingly crushed by circumstances. This is the first jolt in Rastignac's spiritual drama: how can all the senseless and infinite horror of life be overcome? On the other hand, he is subjected to the equally strong influence of the murderer-philosopher Vautrin, who with his ironic critique strenghens Rastignac's growing will to victory. The constant dual action of these two factors—the direct observation of the profound tragedy and involuntary submission to the power of the convict's cynical philosophy—finally forms Rastignac's agressive aspirations.

Raskolnikov is in the same predicament.

Dostoevsky puts him between Marmeladov and Svidrigaylov. First he is plunged into the gloomiest
depths of life's horror, and then he is educated about
super-human power by an inveterate skeptic with
bloody hands. In both cases the tragedy of incipient
Napoleonism, which is not yet strong enough to
reject totally the idealistic strivings of the earlier
period, is caught between two powerful and com-
manding influences: the horrors of life and the
philosophy of hopelessness. Dostoevsky made his
judgement about the whole profound truth of the
inner composition of *Père Goriot* when he made
Raskolnikov run into the drunken Marmeladov and
led him to the too sober Svidrigaylov.

Such are the stages of Raskolnikov's spiritual
drama, which repeat the main phases of Rastignac's
psychological history. But Dostoevsky's hero is
also close to Balzac in the purely theoretical justification of his crime.

VIII

Raskolnikov's decision to kill the old usurer is
based on a whole philosophical system. It is set forth
in his article, and it is developed in detail in his conversation with Porfiry. This is the doctrine of dividing
humanity into two categories with the consequent
sanction of the higher race's right to spill blood.

It is worth noting that Dostoevsky specifically
insisted on the lack of originality in the philosophy
of his novel's hero. "You see that so far there isn't
anything especially new here. This has been printed
and read a thousand times," asserts Raskolnikov,
speaking of his own essay. Razumikhin also notes,
"Of course, you are right to say that this is not new,
and that it's like everything that we have read and
heard a thousand times before."

And in fact, in his first magazine article, using

the rights of one making his literary debut, Raskolnikov allows himself several borrowings. It is a curious coincidence that to structure his theories here Raskolnikov used the pre-death letter of that very same Lucien Rubempré whose first essay inspired Dostoevsky in 1846 to write his humorous feuilleton for Nekraskov's almanac. The essay in *Periodical Talk* which so interests Porfiry Petrovich is expounded almost literally in the pages of the *Human Comedy.*

The content of Raskolnikov's celebrated essay boils down to two propositions:

(1) Humanity is divided into two parts: lower (ordinary) people, and real men, i.e., those who have the gift or talent to say something new in their milieu.

(2) This higher category has the right to step through blood to make its idea victorious. "Lawgivers were set up by humanity," explains Raskolnikov, "beginning with the most ancient, continuing with the Licurguses, Solomons, Mahomets, Napoleons, etc.—every one of them was a criminal just because of the very fact that he set up a new law, thus destroying the ancient one which had been held sacred by society and passed down from their forefathers, and of course, they were not afraid to shed blood if it was blood (sometimes quite innocent blood, bravely shed for the ancient law) which could help them."

Raskolnikov asserts that his essay was written apropos of a book, without, however, naming either the book or its author. But we find the main material for Raskolnikov's essay in Balzac's books. *"The example of Napoleon,* so fateful for the nineteenth century because of the pretensions which he inspired in so many mediocrities, stood before Lucien"—so formulates Balzac (my italics, L.G.), speaking of his hero's drama, a drama resounding with one of the

44

main motifs in *Crime and Punishment.* "I wanted to become a Napoleon, that's why I killed," Raskolnikov formulates the motive for his murder, "I murdered on the example of authority . . . "

In various parts of the *Human Comedy* we find variants of the basic materials for Raskolnikov's essay. Here, for example, is the way Balzac presents the thesis of the two human categories:

"You have sometimes said that Abel has his descendents. In humanity's great drama Cain is the opposition. You descend from Adam in the line into which the Devil continued to pour the fire whose first spark was thrown into Eve. From time to time in this tribe of demons there are terrible, unbridled characters who combine all human strengths and remind one of those furious beasts of the desert whose existence requires vast spaces. Such people are just as dangerous in society as lions in Normandy: they need prey, they devour people from the crowd and feed on the money of fools."

So far this is just the usual romantic challenge to society "which we have already heard and read a thousand times," as Razumikhin asserts after hearing Raskolnikov's essay on the same theme. But here is a closer parallel to his idea.

"If God wills, Moseses, Attilas, Charlemagnes, Mahomets or Napoleons emerge from these mysterious creatures. But when He lets these gigantic forces rust on the bottom of an ocean-generation, they turn into Pugachevs, Fouchiers, Levelles and Abbats Herrera. They are saturated with the poetry of evil."

Here already we clearly perceive Raskolnikov's first dogma about dividing people into "trembling worms" and the power of the possessors—"Napoleons or Mahomets", he repeats after Balzac.

Balzac's subdivision of all humanity into two columns foreshadows not only their categorization according to their basic inclinations towards good or evil, but also their separation into Raskolnikov's divisions of the "ordinary" and the "extraordinary," or, as we would say now, into Nietzsche's "slaves and masters." Balzac definitely puts in Cain's column not only Atilla and Charlemagne, but also Mahomet, Moses and Napoleon. Just as in Dostoevsky, and subseuqently in Nietzsche, everyone feeble and pitiful is put into one traditionally positive category; simultaneously the race of the outcast (or those acknowledged only when they are victorious) is accorded true greatness and superior beauty.

We find further development of Raskolnikov's theory in another Balzac novel:

> Men of genius have no brothers or sisters or parents; the great deeds ahead of them prescribe seeming egotism for them and obligate them to sacrifice everything to their greatness. Genius depends exclusively on itself. It is the only judge of its means, because genius alone knows the ends of these means; *genius must stand above the laws once a person is destined to re-create them;* he who controls his age can possess everything, risk everything, for everything belongs to him ["the destruction of the present in the name of something better," as Raskolnikov says, L.G.] . This truth is proved by the first steps of Bernard Palissi, Louis XI, Fox, Napoleon, Christopher Columbus, Caesar—all the celebrated gamblers, in the beginning poor and misunderstood, who subsequently became the pride of their countries and the whole world. . . . But he who does not attain success commits an unforgivable crime—an insult to society's majesty. After all, a defeated person detracts from all of the acts of civil bravery on which a society rests—society which in horror casts out of its bosom all the Marys who come to the ruins . . . "[7]

"Truths come out of their borning places only to bathe in the blood which refreshes them," asserts Balzac in one of his philosophical stories. "You forget that political freedom, absence of unrest among the people, even science—all these are blessings for

which fate demands a bloody price . . . " Such are
the distant preludes to the *Diary of a Writer* in Balzac's novel. Such is the *Human Comedy's* condoning
of blood on the conscience—something which lies at
the basis of Raskolnikov's philosophical system.

It is with good reason that during his foreign
journey in the winter and spring of 1867, Dostoevsky,
undertaking the literary education of his wife, gave
her *Père Goriot* first. Just three or four months before
Crime and Punishment had been finished. And we
understand why, still under such a fresh impression
of his artistic debt to Balzac, Dostoevsky gave his
wife the story of Eugène Rastignac as one of the
greatest books of European literature.

And, of course, he was not mistaken in his evaluation. The novel which gave impetus to the birth of
Crime and Punishment has a right to considered among
the few immortal books of world literature.

IX

Of course, we are far from having exhausted all
of the questions which arise when comparing the
names of Balzac and Dostoevsky. Such general features of their work as fantastic realism, heightened
interest in maniacal passions, deepened penetration
into the psychology of unbelieving mystics, or the
careful sounding of all the nooks and crannies of a
criminal conscience—all of these could serve as
themes for new comparisons and parallels. They
would confirm and more fully explain the basic
reason for Dostoevsky's exclusive, lifelong attention
to Balzac—the profound creative kinship of the two
writers of different countries and generations. They
would reveal more fully how their works combine
the two antagonistic streams—Christianity and
Paganism, compassion and will to power, humility
and the right to blood—which to the end tore their

work apart.

But though he had one of the strongest influences of anyone on Dostoevsky's artistic development, in no way did Balzac change the profoundly original creative tone of Raskolnikov's creator. *Crime and Punishment,* the concept of which owes so much to Balzac, remains one of the most original, profoundly personal, inimitable works of world literature. Although born in reading of Balzac, in its final form *Crime and Punishment* differed from its prototype so much that at first glance it seems strange to compare the story of Rastignac with Raskolnikov's tragedy and place *Père Goriot* alongside a book which is a veritable distillation of the Faustian "woe of all humanity."

The thread which ties these two novels is lost as Raskolnikov's drama develops. What is most profound, sacred, and vital in *Crime and Punishment* is tied with only a single source—Dostoevsky's soul. This was the source of all the visions, nightmares, and torments of that hot Petersburg week when the most profound questions of the universe were resolved in a bloody act in the soul of one poor student. This was the source—the depths of his spirit which in his youth recognized his own genius; and later, in prison, attracted by the mighty tempering of criminal will, Dostoevsky nurtured his first mystery about fallen and reborn conscience. It was in *Crime and Punishment* that he first combined all of the questions which had constantly tormented him from childhood—redemption of guilt, sin and retribution, purification through suffering and fall, marching to truth through blood, and the torment of rebellion against God. Not even remotely do we discover in Balzac's novel any of these strivings, which raise the detective story to the level of true religious tragedy. Dostoevsky's own words about Pushkin's Byronism could be applied to *Crime and Punishment:* "Imitations never contain such independence of suffering and such depth of self-awareness . . . "

And still Balzac has vast significance in the creation of *Crime and Punishment.* He passed the spark from which the whole fiery pillar of Raskolnikov's tragedy arose. He had already outlined sharply, unforgettably for Dostoevsky, the image of a poor student exhausted by the tormenting moral problem whether one has a right to kill the insignificant to save the life and work of the great.

That, of course, is an immeasurable service.

The early reading of *Père Goriot* was an important event in Dostoevsky's life. In order to understand one of Dostoevsky's greatest creations it is essential to turn to the work of Balzac, as well as to study his first attraction to titanic character types, his later prison impressions, and his ruminations on the gospels.

Balzac and Dostoevsky

NOTES

1. By this time Balzac had already written: *La peau de chagrin* (1830-31), *Gosbeck* (1830), *Jésus-Christ en Flandre* (1830-31), *Le chef-d'oeuvre inconnu* (1831), *Louis Lambert* (1832), *Eugénie Grandet* (1833), *L'Histoire des treize* (1833-35), *Séraphita* (1834), *La Messe de l'athée* (1836), *Le Lys dans la vallée* (1835-36), *La Femme de trente ans* (1830-34), *César Birotteau* (1837).

2. How popular Balzac was in Russia even in the thirties is indicated by the constant references to him even in works of fiction. In the *Son of the Fatherland* for 1836, Part 175, there was a "semi-story" entitled "A Private Matter between Tradesmen" under the transparent initials "F.B." [Faddei Bulgarin, trans.]. It begins with the following dialogue: "I have no intention of leaving the yard," answered the prince, straightening himself on the sofa and putting his book on the table, "this reading has given me the greatest of pleasure." —"And what are you reading?" —*"The Unfortunates* by Balzac, the French Alexander Orlov, in the words of our esteemed journalists. His *Eugénie Grandet* is a charming thing. But it's time to go . . ." In Lermontov's *A Hero of Our Time* we find this description of Pechorin: "He sat there like a Balzac coquette in her overstuffed chair after a tiring ball." (M. Lermontov, *Works,* Edition of Academy of Sciences, IV, 189.)

3. *The Northern Bee,* 1843, No. 161, 172, 200, 214.

4. Champfleury, *"Balzac au collège," Musée universel,* 1873, tome 1, p. 116.

5. Let us quote a passage from one newly-discovered document about Balzac's trip to Russia. It is a coded dispatch from the Russian envoy to Paris, Kiselev, sent July 12/24, 1843; it was preserved in its original form (without coding) in the embassy's book of copies and only recently discovered. It was published by J. W. Bienstock in the article mentioned above *(Mercure de France,* No. 635, 1924). This is its content:

"If M. de Balzac, the novelist, has not yet arrived in Petersburg, he probably will soon be there, for on the 2/14 of
this month he was issued a visa to leave through Dunkirk
to Russia. Since this writer is in constant financial difficulties, and recently he is more pinched than ever, it is extremely possible that one of the goals of his trip is literary
speculation, in spite of the newspaper reports to the contrary. If this is true, playing to M. de Balzac's monetary
needs, one might use the pen of this writer, who still has
a certain popularity here as generally in Europe, to write
a refutation of the repulsive and slanderous book of de
Custine." —A direct description of Balzac's visit to the
Russian Embassy to get his visa is in the diary of the
Russian diplomat Balabin for 1843 and published by
Ernest Daudet.

6. *Time,* July 1862. Apollon Grigoriev, "The
Poems of N. Nekrasov," in "Critical Review" section,
page 43. "Sketches on the Latest Literary Trends in
France," *Time,* March 1862, pp. 149-201. Apollon
Grigoriev, "Famous European Writers Judged by
Russian Criticism," *Time,* March 1861, in "Critical
Review" section, p. 48, p. 58. Dostoevsky, *Works,*
X, 208.

7. We have direct testimony from Dostoevsky himself about his acquaintance with the Balzac novel which
contains this passage. *Lost Illusions* also contains the celebrated feuilleton of Lucien Rubempré which Dostoevsky
tried to imitate in his humorous introduction to Nekrasov's
almanac.

COMPOSITION
IN
DOSTOEVSKY'S
NOVELS

I

Dostoevsky studied the craft of writing long and patiently. Without doubting his calling, long before his first printed works, he learned to pay close attention to the technical devices used by celebrated writers from Gogol to Hugo, diligently employing the finest models to study the rules and laws of verbal art.

The problem of form was the first creative task which stood before him at the start of his literary career. When he was still of school age that solid framework of external composition which protects the internal life of ideas became the main object of his study. Entertaining content, originality of conception, the exciting power of dramatic conflict—all that usually totally grips the attention of adolescent readers could not distract Dostoevsky from this central question: how is it put together? Why does this page excite interest, where does the gripping power of this description lie, how is the striking vividness of this landscape, this character or this dialogue attained—these were the kinds of secrets of the creative laboratory and literary mechanics which primarily interested this seventeen-year-old romantic of the 1830s.

To help answer these questions he turned to specialists' articles and guides. From the theory of literature, literary history, contemporary criticism, and from the memoirs and correspondence of writers he obtained a specialist's knowledge of many case histories, legends, facts, and stories about the miracles wrought by the best creative minds in the course of their exhausting labors. With concealed anxiety, as if sensing the torment which lay ahead on his own path as a writer, he studied attentively this great testimony to the sacrifice and striving of the great verbal warriors who had emerged victors in the battle with indomitable form—often at the price of broken souls, dulled consciousness, and debilitated bodies.

Long after his letters contain reflections of this keen interest in the eternal martyrdom typical of writers' fates. He informed his brother that Chateaubriand reworked *Atala* seventeen times; Gogol worked over *Dead Souls* eight times; Pushkin tirelessly reworked and recast his shortest poems; Sterne covered one hundred quires of paper for his tiny book of journeys; and finally, it was only the lack of reworkings which resulted in such monstrous violations of good taste in the greatest of the great— Shakespeare himself. "Raphael would work on a painting for a year, polishing, touching up, and the result was a miracle!"—that became the guiding slogan of his creative experiments and the watchword of his esthetics.

All of this spurred him on, heightened his ability to work, and gave wings to his quest for future creative achievements. The whole period of his literary formation is marked by this need to study and perfect himself, to constantly widen his artistic horizons and unceasingly enrich himself by mastering the descriptive techniques discovered by all of his great predecessors.

Hence the multitude of varied theoretical and technical data in Dostoevsky's early letters. Questions of form are always foremost for him. He gets interested in the French critic Nisard's essay on Hugo no less than in the poet himself, and the most emotional monologues of Rodrigo or Phaedra cannot distract his main interest from Corneille's structuring his tragedies on Seneca's model. With the same kind of attention to verbal technique and even to questions of meter, he compares Ronsard (unjustly, of course) with Trediakovsky and refers to the "cold rhymster" Malherbe. He gets indignant about the romantics' current disdainful formula "classical form!" and complains to his brother about the latter's statement that the French tragedians are weak in external structure. "Speaking about their form you almost went out of your mind!" he says indignantly to this thoughtless detractor of classicism.

His concerns for language are of the same character. He pays special attention to purity and expressiveness of style, points out to his brother inaccuracies in the latter's translations, begs him not to mix foreign words into Russian texts. It would seem that at the time of his first literary efforts this early admirer of Hoffmann and Balzac, this future bold inventor of neologisms, had not stopped being inspired by the Boileau of his school days:

> Surtout qu'en vos ecrits la langue révérée,
> Dans vos plus grand éxcès vous soit toujours
> sacrée!

Judging by Dostoevsky's early letters one could expect that in his maturity he would turn out to be a writer of academic correctness and classical polish, a writer who would work out his literary projects with mathematical accuracy and hone his style with Flaubertian perserverance. He never stops dreaming of "graphically-good" form in which to embody all of his concepts; he laments the loss of the elevated perfection demanded by the old schools, which were disappearing, and the word *chef d'oeuvre* is never absent from his letters when he is evaluating his own writing or that of others. For each early work he dreams of a flawlessly precise, strict and graceful structure, and of using the most expressive, pure and resonant words. To conquer the beautiful he needs a weapon made from the strongest, most lusterous, most highly tempered and turned steel— with a diamond-covered handle.

How then did this most diligent verbal laborer, this tireless schoolboy *ès-lettres,* this fanatic seeker of literary perfection, this fierce admirer of Pushkin and Racine, work out the unexpected kind of chaotic novel he did, a novel in which alongside the most profound philosophical, religious and social concepts there are disorderly and raw hunks, elements of the newspaper, melodrama, detective story and popular adventure novel.

II.

The conditions of journalistic work and the demands of a literary career gradually lowered the implacable severity of Dostoevsky's youthful set of poetics. In the process of printing and publishing his first works Dostoevsky was forced to take account of the opinions and impressions of those around him, to consciously compromise with the more flexible demands of current journalism, and even, following journalistic requirements, to imperceptively alter his strict theoretical principles. Like the majority of important writers doomed from their first lines to make a living with their pens, isolated innovator though he was, he, little by little began to bring his own capricious manner into line with dominant reader tastes, not, however, ever for a moment losing sight of his hallowed creative ideas.

The school principle of classical perfection worked out over theories of literature and writers' memoirs retreated before the unexpected new thesis suggested to him by journal work. He shifts from his early devotion to the concepts of artistic perfection to the dominant new principle of narrative art: that it be interesting. He now considers it possible to sacrifice all the canons of form and the classical prerequisites of the academy in order to accomplish his main purpose— to strike, intrigue, or stun the reader from the very first lines, and not to let him out of the power of his narrative until the very end.

The narrator must first of all be interesting—

that is Dostoevsky's new axiom, one which displaced the commandments of his earlier theories. "Composing with talent, means composing in an interesting way," he subsequently formulated the main law of literary art, "because the very best book, no matter what else it is or what it discusses, is interesting."

As the years passed, external interest of story became dominant in Dostoevsky's narrative technique. The main theoretical question on which his later creative doctrine turned almost completely was how to insure that the narration grip the most apathetic reader.

This concern for interest of presentation remained with Dostoevsky until the very end. Dostoevsky generously grants his heroes the ability to immediately subject their listeners to themselves. Stepan Trofimovich Verkhovensky utters only the opening sentence of his speech before a noisy and aroused audience which desperately wants some kind of scandal, and immediately he completely possesses them. "The whole hall immediately grew quiet, all looks were turned to him, some with fright. There's no denying it, he knew how to interest people from his first word. Heads even started popping out from behind the curtains in the wings." Fetyukovich begins to speak after the prosecutor's oration, which has produced a very great impression, and "all fell quiet when the first words of the celebrated orator rang out, the whole hall fixed their eyes on him." Another hero begins his story in quite different circumstances, but he attains the same results. "I remember," the raw youth reports, "that somehow I had the gift of beginning to tell a story very cleverly. In an instant terrible curiosity appeared on their faces." One of the listeners "literally fixed her eyes on me."

In all this one senses Dostoevsky's own constant concern with interesting the reader from the first word, and immediately arousing "terrible curiosity." At the beginning of his career he strives to give his stories

Composition in Dostoevsky's Novels

"striking tragic interest"; he wants even to surpass "the interest of a Dumas work," and much later, finishing *The Idiot,* he mourns that the denouement of the novel is not striking enough.

It is remarkable that in his journals Dostoevsky places criminal case histories with popular appeal alongside serious literary and scholarly material. While doing this he considers it necessary to append provocative editorial notes. In one of the issues of *Time* he prints the most detailed account of Lassener's trial with the subtitle "From France's Criminal Trials" and a detailed note designed to excite interest. Like the majority of the editorial notes in the journal it probably belongs to Dostoevsky.

We think it will please the reader if from time to time we print celebrated criminal trials in our journal. Quite apart from the fact that they are more interesting than any conceivable novel, because they illuminate dark sides of the human soul which art does not like to touch upon, or if it does touch upon them, it does so in passing, as an episode; quite apart from this, the reading of such trials, it seems to us, will not be without edification for Russian readers. We think that besides the theoretical discussions which are so often printed in our journals, knowledge of the practical and actual application of these theories to various trials in the West will also be not without use for our readers. We will choose the most interesting trials. We guarantee this. At the center of the trial offered here, is the phenomenal, mysterious, terrifying and interesting personality of one man. Base instincts and cowardice in the face of deprivation made him a criminal, and he dares to present himself as a victim of the age. And all this with limitless vanity. It is a type of vanity taken to its last degree. The trial was conducted in a boldly dispassionate manner, reported with the precision of a daguerrotype, a physiological sketch.[1]

This is remarkable testimony. It turns out that the raw data of stenographic courtroom records have somehow more significant qualities for a reader than the art of a novelist. This kind of record probes more profoundly the psychology of dark passions, reveals

Composition in Dostoevsky's Novels

in life itself the presence of personalities of "phenomenal, mysterious, terrifying, and interesting" natures, and mainly, is "more interesting than any novel." This is the theoretical justification of a typical Dostoevskian device; he made wide use of current, well-known trials when constructing his own novels.

The demand that all kinds of printed material be interesting continued to serve as his guiding principles until the end. Just a few weeks before his death he informs Ivan Aksakov to "make an effort to strike the reader and attract his attention with the first issues" of his new ideological organ. "Make *Rus* more varied and interesting—and intensify this as you go on. Otherwise they'll say: 'intelligent but boring'—and they won't read it." Such is the basic commandment of this old journalist who never forgot his editorial concern for the interest of printed material.

This concern for interest, which spans Dostoevsky's whole literary career, was the prime cause for the destruction of his early theory of prose. Other circumstances played a role too.

In the course of his work as a writer Dostoevsky came to the conclusion that it was necessary for the novelist to liberate himself from all of the constricting canons found in classical theories of art. Reading the literature of romanticism, he was struck by the new school's effort to make the novel a liberated and all-embracing form. The task of achieving a universal and free embodiment of life in all its completeness and variety was obviously at variance with the principles of Raphaelesque "polishing" of themes or exhaustive filtering of life material through the tiny nets of strict literary rules. From the last epigones of romanticism, coming right up to the realistic trends which replaced it, from Hugo, Balzac, and George Sand, Dostoevsky learned just how convenient this new form of "free novel" was, a novel fragmentary in structure and varied in its complement of characters, replete with episodes and disasters, whose endless conflicts open up the greatest possibility for the author to express the totality of his ideas about the world, life and man without preaching or digressions.

This romantic principle of free novelistic form coincided with Dostoevsky's basic creative demand in the mature part of his career. The striving to grasp and fix all life impressions in their original form, without systematizing them, preserving behind their reworked sequence all the fortuitousness, disorderliness and even the absentmindedness of their fragmentary movement in reality—all of this helped to sustain the destruction of the classical principles of his early doctrine.

He gradually developed completely new devices. The striving for sharp contours, fineness of polish, relief of form, and purity of line gave way to a feverish accumulation of spots of paint, daubed shadow and dots of light without concern for transitional shades or the wholeness of the picture. This reflects Dostoevsky's basic requirement to reveal and reflect life not in its finished and polished forms, but in its ever-changing stages of formation, maturation and development.

In his profound dissatisfaction with old models and in his turbulent search for new forms, the question which arose before Dostoevsky was can one make use of all life material without punishment, can one bring it all into literature without reworking it, in raw hunks and undigested sections—but at the same time preserve the artistic significance of the work as a whole.

Dostoevsky gave an unconditionally affirmative answer to this question, and by following this principle he soon solved the main structural difficulty in writing his novels.

III

His composition can be reduced to two basic principles: significance of philosophical idea and interest of the external intrigue.

The starting point of Dostoevsky's novel is the *idea.* An abstract concept of a philosophical character serves him as the central core around which he hangs all the multitudinous, complex and confusing events of the plot. The diversity of the intrigue gives the novel that power of movement and external interest which is especially essential here—in view of the abstract concept which dominates the entire story. The main secret of the whole structure is in the use of interesting external intrigue to compensate the reader for the tiring tension caused by his attention to the philosophical pages.

All of Dostoevsky's novels are structured on this principle. Their primary germ is in an abstract idea of a moral-psychological, religio-philosophical, or socio-political character. This is the core of the novel, uniting all the events of its plot. The problem of the superman-failure in *Crime and Punishment,* the depiction of an absolutely perfect man in *The Idiot,* the psychology of Russian recklessness in *The Gambler,* the spiritual decay caused by revolutionary activity in *The Devils,* the fall and accidental nature of the Russian family in *The Raw Youth,* the path of purification from great sinfulness in the uncompleted *The Brothers Karamazov*—these, in simplified formulations, are the basic ideas which Dostoevsky needed first of all, before beginning work on his novels.

Having set up this philosophical core, Dostoevsky unleashed a whole whirlwind of events around the abstract concept which interested him, not disdaining any of the devices used by penny-dreadfuls to maintain interest.

A murder extraordinary either in its setting or its motives, and all the turnabouts in the subtle duel between investigative power and the actual or supposed murderer *(Crime and Punishment, Brothers Karamazov),* underground activity of conspirators unhinging a whole society with their murders, arsons and scandals

Composition in Dostoevsky's Novels

(The Devils), a fight over an important document,
complicated by all the snares of blackmail *(The Raw
Youth),* the emotions of gambling and the struggle
that goes on at the gaming table *(The Gambler),* the
excesses of dark passion, the fight for a woman, inheritances of millions, murder and madness *(The Idiot)*
—such are the vivid means of heightening narrative
interest in all of Dostoevsky's novels. He was never
stopped by the thought of the cheap sensationalism
of these distinctive raw materials in a novel. He knew
that the low artistic value of separate episodes useful
for awakening and maintaining reader interest could
be compensated for by the profundity of the basic
idea and verisimilitude in character development. He
was certain that the interest of the novel's philosophical idea and the deepening of psychological development would keep the plot from falling to the level of
the popular feuilleton and maintain the whole work
on an artistically significant level.

And in fact the composition of Dostoevsky's
novels, despite its complexity, always does preserve
unity of general impression. Despite the absence of
concern for even and graded arrangement of materials,
despite the great opulence of episodes and side themes—
which Strakhov had already warned the author of
Crime and Punishment about—in Dostoevsky's novels,
all of the separate branches of the story inexorably
lead to its main, central idea; and this unity of internal idea communicates the essential wholeness to the
scattered sequence of events.

But the requirement of making the reader's per-
ception of the philosophical material easier inevitably
leads to Dostoevsky's effort to vary his main theme
constantly, using every means possible to liven up the
story. Above all he gives intensified development to
dialogues, because they dramatize and vivify philosophical ideas with the actual intonations of the human
voice and all the entertaining idiosyncrasies of direct
speech. He also resorts to devices—convergence of

disasters, the frequent change of mysterious or eccentric heroes—which in the area of structure make Dostoevsky's novel traceable to one of its original models: the old adventure novel.

IV

Dostoevsky had a variety of literary teachers. Apart from the pleiad of great instructors from the classical pantheon of world literature, he studied his art using other models. A whole series of now-forgotten writers, who were dismissed by their descendants and literary tradition, figured among his favorite readings.

The works which we arbitrarily designate with the general term "adventure novel" were connected to various literary groups at the end of the eighteenth century and in the first decades of the nineteenth century. Here we have the English Gothic novel, the French *roman-feuilleton* with its pretensions to social confession, and the Russian historical novel of the 1830s. But in all of its branches this literary genre preserves a basic feature—an abundance of episodes and multiplicity of heroes, a piling up of events and endless complication of the intrigue—all of which serve as defining traits of the old adventure novel.

Dostoevsky knew and loved these distant representatives of the *roman d'aventures* of earlier centuries. He was delighted by *Don Quixote,* which remains, in spite of its didactic aim of battle against the literature of chivalry, the typical novel of adventure. He knew and highly valued *Gil Blas,* the whole content of which boils down to a retelling of innumerable interesting adventures. But Dostoevsky's immediate teachers in composition were not so much Cervantes and Le Sage as a whole pleiad of later representatives of "adventure" literature.

Perhaps in the forefront of early nineteenth

Composition in Dostoevsky's Novels

century European novelists one should put the English "horror school" of Gothic novelists—in the person of the direct predecessors of romanticism; Ann Radcliffe, Matthew Lewis, and Charles Maturin.[2] Dostoevsky's later teachers—Hoffmann and Walter Scott, George Sand, Balzac and Hugo also took away many strong impressions from their reading of these first psychologists of terror and satanists of the new literature. But Dostoevsky had first-hand knowledge of them too.

Long before Edgar Allan Poe, who subsequently made such a strong impression on him, in the period of his childhood reading, Dostoevsky found the first sketches of psychological suffering in the old novel of adventures. And no matter how he related to these primitive depictions of horror subsequently, Ann Radcliffe and Maturin played their role in the development of his artistic taste.

The honor of founding the "nightmare school" in the European novel belongs to a woman. The English novelist Ann Radcliffe, who wrote a whole series of fantastic novels at the end of the eighteenth century, is considered the direct predecessor of the later "satanists"—Lewis and Maturin. The early romantics highly valued her main innovative device—the depiction of all the fearsome and dark sides of existence, her exclusive proclivity for the description of crimes, agonies, madness, executions, tortures and all kinds of torments. But the later epigones of romanticism too, those such as Walter Scott, Hugo, Balzac, George Sand, who began the realistic novel, continued to value Ann Radcliffe as a diverting storyteller and inexhaustible inventor of complicated and interesting situations.[3]

In Russia the European adventure novel enjoyed wide popularity at the beginning of the nineteenth century. Evidence of this is provided first of all by catalogues of old libraries, these exhaustive book lists where the simple statistical data on the quantities of editions or the simultaneous appearance of several translations tell us so much about the reading fads and tastes of that distant time.

We learn from them that before 1794 and 1809 fourteen novels of Ducray-Duminil came out, of which many went through three editions. We learn of the readers' interest in Pigault-Lebrun and Lewis, whose names are printed in large print on each translation. But Mrs. Radcliffe enjoyed special popularity. Sopikov lists ten novels by her, i.e., everything that the English novelist wrote, besides which the majority of them went through several editions each. In one of the issues noting the novel *The Monk, or the Deleterious Results of Hot Passions* (St. P., 1802), the assiduous librarian notes in square brackets: "It is well know that Lewis is the author of this book, but to make it sell better the Russian publisher printed it under the name Radcliffe."

This was apparently the best method to guarantee a "big sale" of a book. "Oh, Mrs. Radcliffe," exclaims Prince Shalikov in his *Fruits of Free Feeling*, "why is it I do not possess your divine gift? With what pleasant and enchanting paths you would have led the reader to the discovery of what was seen and heard by my heroine!" And further on in his story this old novelist does not cease his raptures over "the magic brush of the incomparable Mrs. Radcliffe."

This was apparently a general enthusiasm. Characterizing reading tastes of the beginning of the nineteenth century one memoirist remarks: "...No one enjoyed such fame as Mrs. Radcliffe. The *horrific* and *sensibility*—in the final analysis these were the two kinds of writing most to the public's taste. Reading of this type finally took the place of earlier kinds of books..." This witness says that on the covers of the Russian translations of Radcliffe the epithet "famous" was printed beside her name.

Later on Russian journals continued to give Ann Radcliffe such praise. The *Son of the Fatherland* quotes the authoritative response of a popular novelist: "Mrs. Radcliffe," wrote Walter Scott, "has disarmed the critics, and her fame has increased with the publication of *The Mysteries of Udolpho.* The title alone was seductive, and the public eagerly rushed to get the book. In many families the volumes of the novel went from hand to hand; impatient readers grabbed them away from each other, and the universal complaints about necessary business being slowed down because of this book served as the common tribute laid at the feet of the writer's genius..."[3]

Many early readers of this English literature of horrors maintained their sympathies for it for a long time. During the epoch when romanticism was being liquidated, such connoisseurs of modern European literature as Druzhinin and Apollon Grigoriev continued to be delighted by these predecessors of a waning movement. Similarly, in 1849 Druzhinin decided to protest the majestic contempt with which many contemporary writers looked at the horror and fantastic stories. "One can not believe in something improbable and still read a story by Hoffmann or a story by Maturin eagerly, with a trembling heart. With no fear of seeming ridiculous I publicly confess that not long ago I re-read Mrs. Radcliffe's one successful novel, the famous *Les Visions du chateau des Pyrénées.** Her works are still highly valued in England, and in certain chapters of *Consuelo* Sand used the English writer's manner with considerable success. But justice demands we say Mrs. Radcliffe's descriptions of deserted castles, catacombs and horrible events are far more vivid and striking. This kind of scene was the specialty of the author of *The Mysteries of Udolpho.*"[4] Druzhinin ends by saying the novels of Maturin and Radcliffe should be republished with critical surveys of Lewis and Hoffmann (who were close to them in spirit), thus assuring publishers rapid sales and doing a service to readers.

Recalling his childhood readings, Apollon

---

*Actually, one of many novels falsely attributed to Mrs. Radcliffe by French publishers (Paris, 1803). *[Trans. note.]*

Composition in Dostoevsky's Novels

Grigoriev stops on the "magic influence" of Mrs. Radcliffe with special warmth. He notes the quite Rembrandtian coloration of her descriptions, the "nervous sensitivity to the life of shades, visions and ghosts," "the perceptiveness of dark and animal passions."[5] What a kindred school, so close to his own tastes, Dostoevsky found here!

Radcliffe's novels were one of Dostoevsky's first literary impressions. In earliest childhood, before he knew how to read, on the long winter evenings he listened "mouth wide open and dying from delight and horror" to his parents' bedtime readings of Radcliffe's endless novels, which later made him have nightmares. In 1861 he wrote to Polonsky, "How many times from childhood on I dreamt of going to Italy. As early as *Radcliffe's novels, which I read when I was only eight years old,* various Alphonses, Catharinas and Lucias were stuck in my head..." (Italics mine. L.G.) *This* is important evidence. The literary impressions of early childhood are never forgotten. Subsequently in *The Village of Stepanchikovo* he has one of his heroes know Radcliffe's novels very well, and on the last pages of the novel he wrote fifty years later, just before his death, he again recalls the English novelist. To characterize fantastic romanticism of adventures he puts an exclamation about the catacombs of the castle of Udolpho in Fetyukovich's mouth.[6]

The plot of *The Mysteries of Udolpho* has the typical plot of adventure literature. It is the story of a poor orphan given into the care of a vicious aunt and separated from her beloved. Her guardian's mysterious husband turns out to be a robber who has built his robber's nest in the lonely castle Udolpho amid the Appenine mountains. Here he causes his wife's death with tyrannical behavior—and frightens the ward in to a desperate escape from this cursed place of unheard-of horrors. Endless wanderings and unlucky adventures of the poor fugitive in search of her disappeared fiance make up the main content of the rest of the narrative;

her meeting with her lost beloved, marriage, and the beginning of family happiness end the epic of ghastly events.

And if in his last novel Dostoevsky has Fetyukovich be gently ironic about the fantastic inventor of the Udolpho mysteries, there was a time when he, like Apollon Grigoriev, highly valued the Rembrandtian coloration of her descriptions and feverishly reacted to her "nervous sensibility," to the life of shades, visions, and ghosts.

V

At the beginning of the century Ann Radcliffe's fame was shared by the most popular novel of that era—Maturin's *Melmoth the Wanderer.*[7]

This Irish preacher was one of the favorite writers of several of Dostoevsky's literary instructors—Walter Scott, who valued the ghastly fantasies of this "Ariosto of crime," Hoffmann, who refers to him in *The Devil's Elixir,* Hugo, who filled his first novels with epigraphs from Maturin, and Balzac, who called him the greatest modern genius, worthy to stand beside Molière and Goethe. In Russia, Pushkin highly valued the author of *Melmoth* and even put him alongside Byron:

> *The fairytales of the British Muse*
> *Disturb the young maid's dreams,*
> *And now her idol has become*
> *Either the pensive Vampire,*
> *Or Melmoth, the gloomy vagabond...*
> *(Eugene Onegin, III, xii)*

In the note to this stanza from *Eugene Onegin,* Pushkin says, *"Melmoth*—Maturin's work of genius.'' Toward the end of the novel Melmoth figures among the new masks of Onegin, who will perhaps appear before the readers in the last part of the novel "as a Melmoth? a cosmopolitan? a patriot?" (VIII, viii).

Maturin's celebrated novel *Melmoth the Wanderer* was published in Dublin in 1820. It is the Faust theme reworked in the spirit of the adventure novel. One of the first Melmoths, a contemporary of Cromwell, left Ireland where his family had begun, and for a long time lived on the continent, occupying himself with magic, astrology and sorcery. He was early possessed by the "great angelic sin" of intellectual pride, and subsequently he completely subjugates himself to the unbridled quest for forbidden knowledge. Having on his conscience the weight of this first mortal sin, he decides to postpone the moment of his death and the last judgment in any way possible. He bargains with the devil for a life of many centuries, on the condition that he give the devil human souls from time to time. In the interest of his own salvation, Melmoth must increase the number of sins and crimes on earth in any way possible, in order to prepare for his hellish counter-agent the human victims who are the price for the postponement of his punishment. He sets himself a merciless code of maximum hostility to anyone whose sins can ease his own fate, and in his wanderings he never ceases applying the law of "displacement of sufferings"—in his words, a subtle and elevated alchemy capable of transforming other people's criminality into pure gold paid against his own redemption.

Melmoth's existence after his agreement with the devil becomes endless wandering around the greatest sufferings in search of exhausted martyrs who will agree to accept the conditions of the devil's trade in exchange for salvation from unbearable present tortures.

He tempts sufferers of all kinds: the healthy man who finds himself in an insane asylum, prisoners locked in the dungeons of the Inquisition, beggars ready to stifle their own children to save them from the torments of death by starvation. He regularly appears at the death beds of members of his clan, when their vices and sins turn their agony into the most tormenting kind of torture—foreseeing their impending punishment. The collection of unspeakable sufferings remains the main thread of the narrative, and all six volumes of *Melmoth the Wanderer* are an unrelenting epic of horrors and torments.

Despite all of the novel's shortcomings, the qualities which could delight such readers as Pushkin or Balzac, who even called Maturin a genius, are obvious. The amazing richness of fantasy and the inexhaustible inventiveness in the way the basic plot is complicated with interesting side episodes, the sharpening of interest to the intense point where the reader is gripped, the variety of characters and situations, and finally, the scope of conception and the abundance of strong and remarkable ideas, which undoubtedly brings Melmoth closely in line with such universal models as Manfred and Lermontov's Demon (the episode with Immalia)—all this truly reveals the unusual caliber of Maturin's creative gift.

The rich psychology of torture which is described in the novel is especially close to Dostoevsky's artistic manner.

In one of the chapters of the novel, Melmoth draws a picture of what awaits the healthy man—who has landed in an insane asylum accidentally, locked away there by the cunning of his relatives—a picture of the slow loss of his reason as a result of being among the insane constantly. He unfolds before him a complete picture of his inevitably growing insanity, resulting from the pointless and horrible emptiness of his existence among the cries and howls of the madmen; he predicts to him the incipient involuntary desire to share the delirium of the mad in order to get away from his own thoughts, then the terrible doubt in the health of his own mind, then finally the tormenting desire to sink into madness as soon as possible in order to save himself from the excruciating consciousness of his own slow mental death. Melmoth ends this masterfully-written page of psychological torture by comparing the state of a normal man in the atmosphere of madness to the sensations of daring men who hang out over precipices, who in the end are ready to throw themselves into the abyss in order to overcome the intolerable vertigo.

Grigorovich tells us that the young Dostoevsky highly esteemed Maturin and read his novels frequently. This testimony, however, needs qualification. It turns out that along with the books of Hoffman Dostoevsky warmly recommended *Confessions of an English Opium Eater* to his comrades.

In Russia this book came out under Maturin's name—*Confessions of an English Opium User. A Work by Maturin, Author of Melmoth.* (St. Petersburg, 1834). Here Russian booksellers employed a common device of the time—using the name of a well-known popular writer on the book of a little-known one. We have already seen that Ann Radcliffe's name was freely placed on the works of other novelists "for the greater sale of these in Russian." Therefore it is not surprising that in Russia the "Anonymous Story" *Confessions of an English Opium Eater* was attributed to the pen of the popular Maturin. In fact, it was written by Thomas de Quincey.[8]

De Quincey was the author of crime stories and philosophical treatises, among which his study *On Murder, Considered as One of the Fine Arts* was particularly famous, later having influence on Musset, Baudelaire and Oscar Wilde. He is usually compared to the first-class masters of the fantastic and horror tale—Hoffmann, Edgar Allan Poe, Gérard de Nerval. These names are proof enough as to how this

Composition in Dostoevsky's Novels

"amazing fantasist" (as he was called by the critic
for *The Northern Bee*) could attract Dostoevsky.

Therefore it is not surprising that Dostoevsky
recommended reading *Confessions of An English Opium
Eater* so warmly. In this "book of dark content" there
are definite notes similar to the dominant themes of his
own future works.

The characteristic tone can be perceived in the
introduction to the confession. The author offers the
reader the most interesting incident from his whole life
story, but he forewarns him that he will unfold before
him a ghastly picture of human suffering, poverty,
crime and the struggle of mighty passions. However,
he promises to explain the moral purpose of his story
at the end of the book.

An epic of extraordinary adventures begins—flight,
cruel pangs of hunger, a stay in a large and deserted
house, expectation of a murderer, complex money
dealings with usurers, duels and robberies—all these are
just the background for the description of "the extreme degree of suffering and humiliation of which
the human race is capable." One of these pages—the
description of a dark, cold and deserted house in which
an abandoned child and poor man dying from hunger
take shelter—was recalled by Dostoevsky in his *The Insulted and the Injured.*

But the books main interest is in the remarkable
description of the effects of opium. Maturin describes
it as an important and solemn pleasure, as a moment
of inner revelation, as the extreme development and
intensification of the higher and purer spiritual abilities.
It is strongly reminiscent of the aura preceding an
epileptic attack. It is not in vain that the author of the
confession bears witness that he was disturbed by terrifying dreams and a *strange disease* developed in him.

In the opium addict's descriptions we hear echoes
of the confessions of an epileptic.

In his descriptions, pictures of higher bliss are
drawn, of unlimited rapture, voluptuous ecstasy when

it seems that you are floating across a "limitless and calm" lake, or that women in the grip of love, voluptuousness, and wine are bending over you. And then "the angel dries your tears, returns lost joy to the heart, until the new burst of voluptuousness disappears in a fit of horror . . ."

Even more remarkable, even closed to Dostoevsky is the depiction of the feeling of space and time of which De Quincey speaks.

> The feeling of space, and therefore of time, is intensified in the extreme... Sometimes it seemed to me that I had lived 60 or 100 years in one night. One time my dream lasted several thousand years, and occasionally it superceded the bounds of anything that human beings can remember. Each ceremony, each threat, each punishment was accompanied by the idea of eternity, which also deprived me of reason.

This original "Confession" which struck Musset, Baudelaire and Wilde met the young Dostoevsky's artistic requirements. The impression from this little book stayed in his memory long after. The confessions of the addict left as much a mark on his artistic development as the horrors of Ann Radcliffe had.

These forerunners of romanticism who later delighted their distant descendants—Baudelaire and Poe—were among the favorite readings of the adolescent Dostoevsky. From them he learned that even in the unruffled age of Voltaire and Derzhavin the ancient equilibrium had been disturbed by the first efforts of a new literature to depict the mysterious attraction of the human consciousness to the world of the sick and the miraculous.

VI

Aside from the English adventure novel, Dostoevsky found many models of the same genre in his beloved French literature. The French brought several new elements to the English authors' epic of horrors, and to the adventure novel. They put courtroom dramas at the forefront and reproduced court sessions in great detail, introducing a whole series of fantastic incidents into the precise depiction of the trial. With the usual tendency of French literature to sharp antitheses, it strove to constantly develop the plot in two parallel planes—high society and the slums. Oversimplifying and distorting certain ideas of the Romantic school which were already in the air, long before Hugo the French novel-feuilleton develops such combinations of extremes as the charm of ugliness, the honor of prison punishment or the chastity of prostitution. It even develops in full measure that purely romantic cult of sin, vice and crime which does most of all to arouse the reader's interest in a story.

In this eternal concern for the external interest of the narrative, the cleverest French creators of the novel-feuilleton were able to inform the plot with vivid dramatic interest, interspersing the story of all kinds of disasters with lively, sprightly and intriguing dialogues, artfully breaking off chapters at the moments of highest tension in the tragic plot, and giving the overall action an uninterrupted and quickened tempo. Thus at any rate we have the novel-feuilleton in the person of its two most important representatives—Frédéric Soulié and Eugène Sue. They were both well known to Dostoevsky.

These representatives of the popular novel of the time in France—Eugène Sue, Frédéric Soulié, Paul de Kock—were as much favorites of the Russian readers of the thirties and forties as the English Satanists were. In Russia they were read regularly just like Balzac, George Sand and Dumas. While the leaders of the intelligentsia of the time were going deeply into the beckoning perspectives of German philosophy, the masses of readers went for the seductive attractions of the French novel. While the Bakunins and Stankeviches were stuffing themselves with Hegelianism and Schellingism, high society youth and even the provincial misses spent their time reading the slum adventures of the popular Parisian literature. In their early years all of the future classics of the Russian novel were attracted to this literature of adventure.

"At that time *The Count of Monte Cristo* and various 'mysteries' began to appear and I read many of the novels of Sue, Dumas, and Paul de Kock," says Tolstoi in his *Youth.* Along with George Sand and Balzac, Goncharov spent his early years reading all the representatives of the European adventure novel, particularly Ann Radcliffe, Eugène Sue and Frédéric Soulié. His enthusiasm for Sue was so great that a partial translation of *Atar-Gull* was Goncharov's first printed literary work, printed in the *Telescope* in 1842.

Turgenev and the philosophically inclined author of *Russian Nights* gave the same kind of testimony. In *A Nest of Gentlefolk* Varvara Petrovna reads up on Balzac, Eugène Sue and Paul de Kock; and one of Odoevsky's heroes admits her predeliction for the new French novelists—Balzac, Eugène Sue, Frédéric Soulié and George Sand. Odoevsky himself called the *Mémoires du diable* a remarkable book.

The opinion of our first Russian critic confirmed these readers' enthusiasm. Belinsky, who as a matter of principle declared it the duty of the critic to follow the literary tastes of the crowd, gave in to its mood in this case and after brief hesitation acknowledged Paul de Kock one of the most remarkable leaders of contemporary French literature, and Eugène Sue—an elevated and humane talent.[9]

It is not surprising that Dostoevsky with his keen literary impressionability should share this general enthusiasm.

At the very beginning of his literary career, dreaming of translating the world classics, Dostoevsky intends to translate Eugène Sue along with Balzac and Schiller. Sue was incredibly popular in the forties, and the latest books of the French

novelist were confiscated from Dostoevsky during
the search at the time of his arrest in 1847. He
found even more delight in Sue's immediate predecessor and teacher Frédéric Soulié, the inventor of
the novel-feuilleton. His name enjoyed vast popularity among youthful literary circles in the forties. In
his "Page from Reminiscences" [*Collected Works of
A. V. Druzhinin,* VIII (1867), p. xi] , Mikhail Lon-
ginov tells of the happily excited mood of the staff
of the young *Contemporary:* "We had a whole manuscript literature of parodies, epistles, poems and all
kinds of literary jokes. Someone proposed putting
our whole potpourri together on the thread of a
long novel in the manner of Soulié's *Mémoires du
diable* or *Conféssion générale.*"

Grigorovich tells how soon after Dostoevsky's
graduation from engineering school "he was very
fond of the novels of Frédéric Soulié," and that he
was especially delighted by his *Mémoires du diable.*
This fantastic novel written in the spirit of Le Sage's
Le diable boiteux is remarkable in that its very first
pages contain a detailed theoretical manifesto of
popular writing. Dostoevsky, who was delighted by
the *Mémoires du diable,* must have remembered this
passage well. Subsequently, introducing into his
novels the most primitive and shocking effects from
folk farces and puppet shows, he was often simply
obeying the witty commandments of the father of
the popular novel and totally relying on his authoritative experience.

Soulié's address to beginning writers opens:

Oh, you young people, you have dreamed only of the
elevated work of geniuses, the pure and holy singing of the
most beautiful voices in the world, of honest and profound
revelation of the truth—you are mistaken, young people, you
are cruelly in error. When you ask the public's attention for
your candid and beautiful speeches, you will see how it rushes
to listen to the coarsest stories of the most trivial authors, the

spectacular news from crime reports. You will see how this old debauchee will start making fun of the chastity of your muse and begin to shout at it, "Oh, you slut, go to hell, or else say something to interest me! I need strong devices to arouse sensation in a benumbed sensibility." "Now listen," says the reader to the author then, "do you have a supply of wild incest and monstrous betrayal, stunning orgies of crime and passion, ones which it is even difficult to convey? If not, shut up right now and go live out your days in poverty and oblivion." Do you hear this, young people? Poverty and oblivion—that's not what you are striving for, is it? So what do you do? You take a pen, a piece of paper and you write on it this title: *Memoirs of a Devil.*

This was one of the lessons which the contemporary French novel taught the youthful Dostoevsky. At the time when his literary technique was being formed this novel, totally devoted to a depiction of the darkest horrors and disasters, robberies, baseness, incest and murders was among his favorite books. And the impression it made on him was so great that even in Dostoevsky's last novel one can still hear echoes of it. In places Ivan Karamazov's devil is undoubtedly done in the style of Soulié's demon. The general tone of the speech of the two devils is identical. The devil of the *Mémoires* parodies the Bible, cites Diderot and Juvenal, Madame de Staël, Malebranche and Voltaire. With sarcastic calm, and rather bored, he makes fun of the world, humans, the person he is talking to, and himself, juggling well known facts in order to unexpectedly reveal a strange kind of seriousness, at times even sad inspiration, and then again to return to his bored irony.[10]

Soulié's immediate student, Eugène Sue, achieved the greatest virtuosity in this literary genre. There were many features of his novels which were bound to interest Dostoevsky in the strongest possible way. Above all there is the eternal theme of poverty in the big cities, and then there is the traditional romantic mixture of fantasy with reality, which in *The Wandering Jew* is reflected in the strange idea of putting the resurrected figures of Salome and Ahasuerus in nineteenth-century Europe.

Subsequently we find a whole series of other features and ideas of Sue in Dostoevsky's novels and stories. Mordant criticism of Catholicism and polemics with the Jesuits, the apotheosis of Napoleon, depictions of night-time orgies among the proletarians in the capitals, justification of any crime as the inevitable product of social inequality—these are among the basic themes of Sue's novels. Among his characters we find the poverty-stricken step-mother sending off her sixteen-year-old ward to sell her body (Madeleine and La Louve), runaway prisoners capable of monstrous treachery (Chourineur), heroically noble sinners (La Goualeuse), epileptic marquises (d'Harville), counts committing forgery (Saint-Remy) and decrepit voluptuaries dying in convulsions of old-age sexual desire (the notary Ferrand).* Is it necessary to remind ourselves of the parallels in Dostoevsky—Katerina Ivanovna sending her step-daughter Sonya out to work in the streets, Fedka the Convict, Nastasya Filippovna and her epileptic prince, Father Karamazov or Princes Valkovsky and Sokolsky committing all kinds of forgeries and crimes.

But the author of *Poor Folk* had to be particularly attracted by the quasi-social tendencies of this literature. Popularizing the ideas of Fourier, Saint-Simon and Owen, Eugène Sue constantly pretended to the calling of a social tribune and social reformer. He succeeded in attaining this calling far beyond the borders of France. [11] If such journals as *Démocratie pacifique* referred to Sue as a fiery defender of democratic ideas, a new law-giver and a

---

*All of the characters enumerated here appear in one novel—*The Mysteries of Paris.* (Translator's note.)

most worthy colleague of J.J. Rousseau, is it surprising that in Russia Belinsky took the popular epics of this clever story-teller for serious efforts at a social novel, and that in his state of exaltation the young Dostoevsky intended to translate Sue's *Mathilde* along with *Eugénie Grandet?*

In any case, this will not go unpunished for him. *The Insulted and the Injured, Crime and Punishment,* even *The Devils* are still colored with the tones of *The Mysteries of Paris* in some passages.[12]

VII

The historical novel, which was created by the romantic school, was extraordinarily close to this old adventure literature. Its greatest representatives, Sir Walter Scott and Hugo, were warm admirers of adventure literature. One of the first Russian historical novelists, Zagoskin, was brought up on Ann Radcliffe.

Thus, apart from direct knowledge of the authors of *The Mysteries of Udolpho* or the fantastic *Conféssions,* Dostoevsky continued to be educated in their school when reading *Ivanhoe, Notre-Dame de Paris,* and even Zagoskin's *Yury Miloslavsky.* The historical novel, which replaced the adventure novel, continued to develop the narrative techniques of the earlier genre.

In his early period Dostoevsky highly valued Sir Walter Scott. He read him while still in his first boarding school and later made his early heroines— Nastenka in "White Nights" and Netochka Nezvanova—read the author of *Ivanhoe.*

These enthusiasms are understandable. The Scottish novelist has many features which should meet Dostoevsky's strongest sympathies.

Above all we have here Walter Scott's mystique of the middle ages, his faith in the miraculous, his mysterious stories about phenomena of "second sight," all of the demonology and magic in his novels. He was virtually the first to inform the action of a novel with dramatic character, and he gave his admirers numerous examples of that lively, varied, flexible and expressive dialogue which was fated to displace the former long descriptions, introductions and authorial explanations.

Perhaps Dostoevsky's rare art in handling dialogue finds its beginnings in the school of Walter Scott. [13]

But far more significant was his enthusiasm for Victor Hugo, which continued until late in his career. It was not limited to the French poet's historical novels, but embraced his works almost totally.

In engineering school Dostoevsky read the poems and early novels of Hugo, apparently leaving unread only the plays—"Victor Hugo, except for *Cromwell* and *Hernani,*" he informs his brother of his readings. He proclaims the author of the *Odes* and *Ballades* the greatest lyric, with "purely angelic character, with a Christian, youthfully-innocent direction in his poetry," something with which neither Schiller, nor Shakespeare, nor Byron, nor Pushkin can compare. He concludes, "Only Homer, with the same indomitable confidence in his calling, with the childlike faith in the god of poetry whom he serves, resembles Hugo in the direction of his poetry."

This enthusiasm is manifested in the later period too. In the first issues of his first journal, *Time,* Dostoevsky begins to print a translation of *Notre-Dame de Paris.* Traveling abroad in 1862, according to Strakhov, he gulped down two or three volumes of the just-published *Les misérables* in one week. In 1876 he makes Hugo's *chef d'oeuvre The Last Day of A Condemned Man* his model and proclaims the psychological etude of the French novelist "the most realistic and truest of everything that he has written."

In many respects Hugo's ideological proximity to Dostoevsky is obvious. The themes of "poor folk" (Hugo has a poem entitled *Les pauvres gens,* written after Dostoevsky's novel), "the insulted and the injured," protest against capital punishment, rehabilitation of criminals, and finally the preachment of universal brotherhood—all of these introduce social motifs into Hugo's and Dostoevsky's novels and supply them with the richest possible material for psychological studies.

But Dostoevsky paid no less attention to the complex architectonics of Hugo's novels. He saw the author's basic striving to arouse the reader's keen interest in the theme and constantly hold his attention in a state of extreme tension. He noted all of the means directed toward attaining this main goal—the thickening of colors, the infinite exaggerations, the play of contrasts, the introduction of antithesis not only into the style but into the plot and characters, the constant sequence of exceptional effects, the piling up of extraordinary adventures and unexpected disasters, and finally, the vast number of heroes, collected from the most contradictory social circles, thus opening up broad possibilities for the author to alternate the most varied novelistic situations with incredible speed.

The mixture of all kinds of narrative elements in *Les misérables*—historical pages on Waterloo, the Revolution of 1830, the depiction of convicts, detectives, prostitutes, bishops in the first ages of Christianity, poverty-stricken dreamers preaching the cult of Napoleon (the general psychological picture of Raskolnikov is strongly reminiscent of the hero of *The Damned,* Ponmercie), and finally the variety of settings—prison, the monastery, the huge city, the Paris tavern, factory centers, the field of battle—all of this continued to show Dostoevsky the necessity of infinitely varying the setting, action, and heroes in novels which set as their goals philosophical tasks such as the depiction of the roads from evil to good, from injustice to truth, etc.

Nurtured on the models of Sir Walter Scott, the Russian historical novel of that period continued to insinuate the same principles of interesting narration into the poetics of Dostoevsky. Zagoskin and Lazhechnikov were part of the program of family readings of the staff doctor [Dostoevsky's father, *trans.*] of the Mariinsky Hospital at the very beginning of the thirties. Ten years later Dostoevsky refers to his story "Roslavlev" in a respectful tone. The plot of the celebrated *Yury Miloslavsky* boils down to a typical depiction of those innumerable obstacles which the comrade in arms of Prince Pozharsky has to overcome in order to marry the boyar's daughter, Kruchinaya-Shelonskaya. This is the usual core of the old adventure novel, and in particular this is the Russified plot of *The Mysteries of Udolpho*, which Zagoskin had read in his youth. [14]

But within our own literature of the beginning of the last century Dostoevsky was especially attracted by one of the greatest representatives of the Russian adventure novel.

Among Dostoevsky's teachers was that half-forgotten writer whom Belinsky called the father of the Russian novel—the author of *A Russian Gil Blas*—V. Narezhny.

Just the title of his most important work, put together on the model of Le Sage's celebrated novel, openly points to the dependency of this Little Russian epic on the European adventure novel. In the words of a scholar writing on Narezhny's works, "the adventure novel" had its most notable reflection in his works; they had an endless variety of the most fanciful and improbable adventures, with a multitude of side characters and an extremely complicated love intrigue.

Composition in Dostoevsky's Novels

Following the Western models, in his long novels Narezhny makes it his task to depict people of the most varied types and social categories. Towards this goal he keeps several parallel plots going in the novel, as if uniting a group of dissimilar stories through the adventures of the main hero. The opening plot branches into countless new episodes, and the fates of the characters get confused in a growing series of all kinds of adventures.

Dostoevsky read Narezhny when he was still a schoolboy, when, according to his brother, he repeatedly re-read Narezhny's *The Seminarian.* It is a very typical adventure novel from the beginning of the century. Abductions with disguises, robber bands, battles, uprisings, flights, unexpected encounters, coincidences and meetings, lost children who unexpectedly find their parents, lovers driven away, cursed by their fathers—these are the main materials on which the numerous episodes are built. Throughout his whole story the author never ceases arousing the reader's attention by provocative forewarnings and emphasizing the sensational elements.

"The events of this day were so fantastic for me that my head began to spin . . . " "At this time minds began to vacillate from political infection. First secretly, and then openly people began to say in the bazaars, in taverns and in seminary classes that the hetman . . ." "Now I will begin the description of one of the most important events in my life, which had a great influence on subsequent happenings." —These are examples of the forewarnings to the reader about impending disasters which are one of the most characteristic traits of Dostoevsky's own narrative technique.

But the most typical feature of the adventure novel is at the center of the basic plot in *The Seminarian*—the theme of the lost child who is found. The main hero, Neon, just before the death of his step-father, the Deacon Varukha, learns that he is not the priest's own son. Toward the end of the novel, after countless troubles and adventures, when the unfortunate Neon stands before the awesome hetman's court waiting for a cruel sentence, it is unexpectedly revealed that he is the grandson of his judge, i.e., the son of the hetman's daughter, who ran away from her father and was long ago cursed by him. On the last pages of the novel before he dies the old hetman, exhausted and growing weaker, rushes to look at his children for a last time after a twenty-year separation, in order to finally forgive the daughter the sin of her disobedience. In the final denouement it turns out that Neon's first youthful love—the beautiful Melita—is his own sister, and his wife, Neonila, is forced to go through an analogous scene of reconciliation with her angry father.

Such were the novels which Dostoevsky had as his reading during the thirties and forties. Later on he maintained a sympathetic attitude to some of them. The company of his literary teachers was always characterized by its diversity, and alongside the classical names he placed those narrators of extraordinary adventures who did not cease to turn his literary tastes and his creative inclinations in the direction of melodrama.

In his own works he often refers to this variegated literature ironically, and in passing he occasionally even attempts to parody some of its typical features. In his first story, *Poor Folk,* he makes fun of popular Russian novels, those "Italian Passions" or "Ermaks and Zuleikas" with their fulsome passages: " 'Countess,' he cried, 'countess!.. All your husband's blood will not cool the madly throbbing ecstasy of my love'!" In *The Village of Stepanchikovo* he makes an ironic reference to the novels which were thrown together in Moscow during the 1830s under such hysterical titles as *Ataman Bur* and *The Sons of Love, or, The Russians in 1104.*

And nevertheless some features of this literature, or literature very close to it, are undoubtedly
typical of his own work. The enthusiasm for Maturin, Soulié or Sue did not go unpunished. At the
high price of involved complications and obvious
sensational effects in his own pages, Dostoevsky
will pay for his delight with *The Mysteries of
Paris* or *The Memoirs of a Devil.* To the end his
philosophical novel will not be completely free of
many flourishes of the feuilleton epic of popular
novelists, and all of the metaphysical pro and contra of his theological disputes will not remove
from his basic plot those complicated and mysterious adventures which turn us back to Ann Radcliffe
and Frédéric Soulié.

VIII

What are the marks of this older novel literature on Dostoevsky's work? And can we precisely
tabulate these distant reflections of his youthful
reading on the later pages of a completely formed
writer?

In the area of composition in his novels these
elements of the old literature of adventures can be
established with a fair amount of precision. Of
course, we do not find in Dostoevsky palace catacombs or hidden doors, or black capes and wide-
brimmed hats, or daggers and poison, in a word
nothing from that operatic ballast from the melodrama which Scott, Hugo and Balzac still sometimes
attempted to use in their novels. But if all of these
decorations and props found no application in the
depiction of the Russian milieu in the middle of the
last century, almost all of the other features of the
novel-melodrama went into Dostoevsky's works.

First of all he reproduced—the only time this
happened in the whole history of the Russian classical

novel—the typical plots of adventure literature. The traditional outlines of the European adventure novel often served Dostoevsky as sketches for the structuring of his intrigues.

He even made use of the stereotypes of this literary genre. In the heat of work for deadlines he was seduced by the commonplace types of adventure plots grabbed up by popular novelists and feuilleton writers. He knew that in his hands, by means of more profound psychological studies and vivid dialogues, this low-caliber material would be elevated to the level and significance of the best models of novelistic literature.

He also used the most characteristic type of novel-feuilleton. A good-for-nothing, who has a glorious title and features of demonic beauty seduces a modest girl, robs her of her property and casts her to the whim of fate. The poor girl, abandoned by the villain-lover and cursed by a stern father, is engulfed in poverty, gets consumption, goes out of her mind and wanders through the noisy and indifferent streets of a metropolis begging alms with a child in her arms. Soon she dies from exhaustion and grief, without having vengeance on the aristocratic good-for-nothing and without forgiveness from her merciless father. Having learned of his daughter's agonies, however, he relents and hurries to her with words of forgiveness, but he gets there only to find a cold corpse. A new epic begins for the poor little girl child, one filled with dark persecutions and miraculous windfalls—beatings, diseases, forced sellings into houses of ill repute and unexpected salvation, until finally in the denouement it is revealed that the unhappy beggar girl is the daughter of a famous prince who it turns out is also, to top all of the unexpected events, the legal husband of her late mother. Such is the plot of *The Insulted and the Injured.*

A slight change in the combination of these

elements and a new plot results. Again the poor little girl, again the attic, disease, madness, tragic death of the consumptive mother, and alongside this princely rooms and a whole net of unexpected coincidences interlocking these two extreme poles of life in the capital. In the center a ruined talent, a mad artist, a poet or a vagabond musician, an unacknowledged genius in his attic overcome by megalomania, and around him ridicule; and the main kernel of the plot is complicated by the unexpected discovery of old forgotten letters which reveal even more vital secrets. Such is the outline of the unfinished *Netoch-ka Nezvanova.*

Dostoevsky made use of these types of popular novel in the latter part of his career too. Even in his last novels he resorts to his characteristic device of outlining the external fates of his most profound psychological figures using the traditional contours of the melodrama.

In this respect the fate of the mysterious "Prince Hal"—Stavrogin—is extremely interesting. The main outline of his life is lifted from the ordinary canvas of the melodrama. A villain, an aristrocrat, rich and handsome, given the seductive features of demonism, he shines in the guards and in high society in the capital. But his gambling, public insults of society women and cruel duels lead him to court and demotion into the ranks. Having served his punishment he again appears in the capital, but in the filthiest slum taverns among the beggars, drunks, and worst refuse of the capital's populace. Here the aristocrat finds himself a wife who is a poverty-stricken cripple and idiot. Then after a period of mysterious absence, he again floats to the surface of society, although he secretly continues to maintain his ties with a runaway convict. At his order this bandit cuts the throat of people he doesn't like and burns down whole sections of town while the one who has given the order, like a new Nero, admires the burning town in the middle of an orgy of love.

No matter what profound philosophical significance the image of Stavrogin attained in his final
development, his whole external history reeks of
the popular novel, the penny-dreadful. Many facts
in the life of the main hero of *The Devils* as if re-
produce the adventures of Rudolph in *The Mysteries
of Paris.* Sue's hero is quite typical. Imperious, a
prince, rich, intelligent, heroically energetic and
strong, possessed of amazing power of will and
herculean muscles, he disdains the love of high society lionesses and the respect of the strong of the
world, lowers himself into the bottom of the under-
world of the capital, where he finds a kind of strange
satisfaction in friendship with a former convict and
a poor prostitute. The novel-feuilleton, as we see,
played its role in the composition of *The Devils.*

It would seem there is not a single feature of
the old adventure novel which Dostoevsky did not
use. Apart from mysterious crimes and mass disasters,
titles and unexpected inheritances, we find here the
most typical feature of the melodrama—aristocrats
wandering through the underground and their com-
radely fraternity with the dregs of society. Stavrogin
is not the only Dostoevsky hero of whom this is true.
It is equally characteristic of Valkovsky and of Prince
Sokolsky and even partly of Prince Myshkin. One of
them even turns out to be virtually a counterfeiter:
"I am a criminal and am participating in the counter-
feiting of false stock certificates for the *** Railroad,"
says this representative of an ancient princely family,
stunning his interlocuter, who is no more prepared for
this kind of confession than the reader of the novel.

We also find in Dostoevsky the precipitate,
catastrophic ending to a complex and cumbersome
plot. With its abundance of horrors and deaths, the
denouement of *The Devils* outdoes even the bloodiest
melodramas. A fire in half the town, three people
stabbed in a half-burned house, the underground

murder of Shatov, the mysterious murder of Fedka
the Convict, the public murder of Liza Drozdova by
the infuriated crowd, Kirillov's suicide, Stavrogin's
suicide, and finally, the natural death of the father
and unwitting patriarch of all these "devils"—Stepan
Trofimovich—it would seem that only Shakespeare
ever allowed himself such a quantity of corpses in
a work without suffering for it.

The reproduction of the main features of the
adventure novel was not limited to this. Dostoevsky
introduced other characteristic devices into his narrative—overhearings of important and mysterious
conversations, often even through neighboring apart-
ments (Svidrigaylov, Dolgoruky), possession of scan-
dalous documents which invisibly link a whole series
of mutually hostile characters (*The Raw Youth*),
involuntary initiations into as yet undisclosed crimes,
public scandals, duels (Stavrogin, Zosima), sudden
faintings, epileptic attacks and even unexpected
slaps in the face—all with the same goal of artificially
intensifying the interest and liveliness of the
narration.

This last device, which goes back to the most
primitive kind of folk puppet shows and other per-
formances, is definitely misused by Dostoevsky. The
slap in the face (which Prince Myshkin gets from
Ganya Ivolgin, Stavrogin from Shatov, Verkhovensky from Fedka, Versilov from Prince Sokolsky,
Dolgoruky from Boring) usually marks a new stage
in the confused novel intrigue sharply—or it is a
saving *coup de théâtre* during complex scenes which
require an intensified change of effects.

In the old novel, as in the eighteenth-century
drama, the names of the heroes designated their
moral characteristics. For example, among
Narezhny's heroes there are Serdobolins ["Heart-
ache"], Chestons ["Honor"], Pravdolyubovs
["Truthlover"], Petimetrovs ["Petit-maître"], Prince
Promotaylov ["Wastrel"], and Countess Modnikova

Composition in Dostoevsky's Novels

["Fashionable"]. However strange it may seem, Dostoevsky introduced this device from the adventure novel into his composition too. His characters' names also reveal their character. It is not difficult, of course, to see in *Razumikhin* the positive practical man, in *Raskolnikov* the rebel and protester diverging from generally accepted norms, in *Lebezyatnikov* a useless banality, in *Svidrigaylov* some kind of shaggy, prurient satyr, in *Prokharchin* a humiliated, downtrodden and pitiful outcast, in *Karamazov* a shade of Eastern stagnation, in *Smerdyakov* all the vileness of human nature. Dostoevsky went even further in the application of this out-moded device of old-time literature in *The Idiot* and decided to name the student "who was by conviction a materialist, an atheist and a nihilist" *Kislorodov* ["Oxygen"], and in *The Brothers Karamazov* the teacher of history *Dardanellov*.

Finally, in his novels he widely applied the device typical in adventure literature of joining contrasts—juxtaposition of spiritual goats and sheep, holy men and sinners, villains and heroes. This led to his tendency, following the example of the older novelists, to depict exceptional types of heroes. In each of his novels one feels this constant propensity of his to depict extraordinary character types. By his own confession in *The Idiot* he strove to depict "a positively beautiful man" and *The Brothers Karamazov* in its unfinished whole would be the description of the life of a "great sinner."

For all of their psychological complexity Dostoevsky's heroes are characterized by extremely elementary features: Raskolnikov, Fyodor Karamazov, Rogozhin, Verkhovensky—they are all bearers of one idea or passion, all to a greater or lesser degree maniacs and men with an *idée fixe*.

We do not find the strange maniacal quality of Dostoevsky's heroes in Tolstoi or Turgenev, or in Goncharov or Chekhov. Soft, muted, vague tones in the twilight spiritual worlds of the Russian

Composition in Dostoevsky's Novels

Hamlets, the soft-hearted and soft-bodied Lavretskys, Oblomovs, Bezukhovs—all of the halftones of their indecisive, vacillating, changeable reflections and deeds—are a complete opposite to the fatalistic outbursts of Dostoevsky's possessed heroes.

This is a feature which is in the highest degree original and unusual for Russian literature. In Dostoevsky's work it is obviously of foreign origin. The villains and victims, criminals and sufferers, unhappy children lost and miraculously found, the "elevated courtesans" purified from sin by suffering and love, the celebrated "Ophelian melodramas," the mad fiancees, mourning their disappeared husbands-to-be (Lebyadkin)—in their basic characteristics all of these figures go back to the old English and French adventure novel. There is no reason for us to expatiate here on the miraculous transformation which they underwent under Dostoevsky's pen.

IX

No matter what respect one has for Dostoevsky's work, one must admit this unexpected fact. In their architectonics, his greatest creations came out of the old adventure novel; and it remains for us only to try to solve the puzzle which involuntarily arises: how do we explain this strange predilection of a great writer for a literary genre bordering on melodrama? How did it happen that the lowest genre of writing art turned out to be the most convenient expression for the creative ideas of an artistic philosopher who was a genius?

There are several reasons. First of all, with its interest in plot the adventure novel was a brilliant solution to a basic problem of Dostoevsky's creative poetics. He created models of gripping narrative interest unparalleled in all of classical literature, and by so doing satisfied his main requirement in the area of novelistic technique.

At the very beginning of his career Dostoevsky

read the latest examples of European literature; he knew that in his time the novel, which embraced all spheres of thought—tragedy, philosophy, history and religion—had to be interesting externally because of its vast internal complexity. He comprehended that the difficult path ahead of the reader through the labyrinth of theories, characters, and human relations included in one book should be made easier for him in every way—by the liveliness and interest of the plot. Throughout his career he never ceased devoting great efforts to solve this complex task, constantly recalling his youthful enthusiasm for the novels of Radcliffe and his youthful delight in the *Memoirs of a Devil.*

He found one other hidden quality in the novel-feuilleton. This was that spark of sympathy, smouldering under thick layers of ash and trash, for the insulted and the injured, sympathy which one feels behind all of the adventures of beggars who get lucky and abandoned babies who are found. No matter what the goals of the authors of melodramas who turned to slums, prisons and hospitals, they did prepare the road for the future social novel. In its idea Dostoevsky's *Poor Folk* is perhaps just as obliged to the sermons of compassion in Sue and Soulié as it is to the humanistic philosophies of all the philanthropists and utopians of the beginning of the century.

And finally, vastly expanding the usual limits of the old novel, introducing into this defined literary genre all kinds of innovations ranging from philosophical doctrines to puppet-show effects out of the folk theater, Dostoevsky satisfied in part his eternal quest for new form. Among the plots and violent deaths, in the atmosphere of crime and scandal, among convicts, criminals, prostitutes, beggars, princes, eccentrics and madmen, he found extensive possibilities to fix onto these many fleeting phenomena of reality all that was strange, extraordinary, and beyond the bounds of everyday life. In all elements of the melodrama which made up

Composition in Dostoevsky's Novels

Dostoevsky's usual plot, apart from the main goal
(to strike and attract the reader) the essential feature of all of his work was clear: a striving to make
the exceptional part of the very body of the ordinary,
to merge them into one, following the romantic
principle; the elevated should be joined with the
grotesque, and by imperceptible transformations
he wanted to take the characters and phenomena
of everyday reality to the limits of the fantastic.

Hence all of the most original aspects of the
complex combinations which we find in *The Idiot,
The Devils, The Brothers Karamazov.* Dostoevsky's
novel is a philosophical dialogue expanded into an
epic of adventure; it is the *Phaedo* put at the center
of *The Mysteries of Paris,* a mixture of Plato and
Eugène Sue.

Composition in Dostoevsky's Novels

NOTES

1. "Lassener's Trial. From France's Criminal Trials," *Time,* No. 2 (1861), section 2, page 1.

2. There are several versions of the latter writer's name in our literature. In Russia he has been called "Matyuren," "Matyurin," "Mechurin," etc. We have used the spelling closest to the English pronunciation.

3. A work devoted specially to the "novel of horrors" recently appeared in France. It is the Sorbonne dissertation by Alice M. Killen, *Le roman terrifiant; ou, roman noir de Walpole à Anne Radcliffe et son influence sur la littérature française jusqu'en 1840* (Paris, 1924). The author traces the family tree of the horror novel, the "gothic novel," or the "black novel" back to the middle of the eighteenth century when Smollett's *The Adventures of Ferdinand, Count Fathom* (1753), and the anonymous *Longsword* (1762) appeared [*Longsword* was written by Leland, *trans. note].* The final date that should be considered the birth of the new genre is 1764, when Horace Walpole's *The Castle of Otranto* was published. The genre is firmly defined in Clara Reeve's *The Old English Baron,* and in the persons of Ann Radcliffe and Matthew Lewis a school is formed. In the 1790s the "horror novel" outlives its epoch of efflorescence. A characteristic device of all of the representatives of the movement is the explanation of mysterious horrors by means of visions and dreams. "After Clara Reeve, in Ann Radcliffe, and then almost all of the novelists of this genre, dreams occupy an extremely important place. Great misfortunes, past and future crimes, are frequently revealed in a terrifying or a sad dream. The premonition of danger frightens no less than the beginning of the danger itself." In particular Lewis creates striking effects with the aid of nightmares "filling with dark premonitions the consciousness of the person who is thus warned about impending danger."

4. "A Letter from a Subscriber in Another City," April 1869. Druzhinin, *Works,* VI, 112-13.

5. Apollon Grigoriev, "My Literary and Moral

Wanderings," *Epoch,* May 1864, p. 140.

6. *The Mysteries of Udolpho* (London, 1794)—one of the most popular Radcliffe novels. Leskov was also among the Russian writers who were enthusiastic about her.

7. At the beginning of the thirties the *Library for Reading* published a review from an English journal of the early novels of Victor Hugo, a review which juxtaposed them with the works of Maturin. In this translated essay from *The Edinburgh Review,* entitled "On Current French Literature," among other things it was said: "Like our English Maturin he [Hugo] in his *Hans of Iceland* has exhausted and over-exhausted all the horrors of Scandanavia. His *Bug Jargal,* a story from the times of the Saint Dominique uprising is quite incredible . . . Hugo's only whole work is without doubt *The Last Day of a Condemned Man"* (*Library for Reading,* Part I, 1834, Foreign Literature, pp. 67-80). In another issue the same journal applies the following formula to the works of Maturin: "His horror was elegant, and with inhuman cold-bloodedness he loved to unearth the deepest secrets of the heart" *(Library for Reading,* VII, 1834, Literary Chronicle, p. 22).

8. See M. P. Alekseev, "F. M. Dostoevsky and De Quincey's Book," *Scholarly Notes of Odessa High School,* II (1922), 97-102.

9. L. N. Tolstoi, *Works,* 1903, I, 319; P. N. Sakulin, *From the History of Russian Idealism. Prince V. Odoevsky* (Moscow, 1913), II, 123, 373; Belinsky, *Works* (Vengerov edition), III, 430; I. Goncharov, "Second Autobiography. First Autobiography," *Russian Past,* CLXVIII, X, 37.

10. Here is a characteristic example of his dialogue: —"Have you ever read Molière?" —"Satan, you are ill using my patience!" —"But still, have you ever read Molière?" —"Yes, I have read him, and re-read him many times." —"Well, if you have read him and re-read him many times, have you ever noticed that the joking poet possessed the most serious thought of his age? Have you ever noticed that this writer, who spoke about everything using such raw expressions was the most chaste soul of his time? Have you ever noticed that the amusing ironist had the saddest heart of his age?"

Composition in Dostoevsky's Novels

11. In an essay on Eugène Sue, Valerian Maikov, noting all of the French novelist's shortcomings and the noticeable decline of his talent in his last novels, gives this curious evaluation of his *The Mysteries of Paris:* "The author of *La Salamandre* made it his task to depict in a broad frame *the whole abyss of misfortunes which hang over the heads of the deprived classes, who are shelterless before the law, their children* deprived of education, to depict the retarded, the sick, the *whole numberless brotherhood of sufferers . . ."* (My italics. L.G.)

12. Newly published materials confirm the length of Dostoevsky's attraction for several writers whom he read in his youth, in particular Sue. E. A. Shtakenshneider in his diary of 1884 [*Voice of the Past* (1916), II, 80] quotes data indicating Dostoevsky's positive attitude to Eugène Sue in the seventies. "Dostoevsky's favorite writer was Dickens, but he still loved and often recommended that I read *Gil Blas,* Sue's *Martin . . .* Sue also has similarities with Dostoevsky, singer of the insulted and the injured . . . " Here it is interesting to note Dostoevsky's interest in the Sue novel in which the favorite theme of adventure literature is worked out—the lost and found child—a theme partially reflected in the plot of *The Insulted and the Injured.*

13. In his remarkable autobiographical fragment "Petersburg Dreams in Verse and Prose," printed in *Time* in 1861 and reprinted in *Russian Thought* (January 1916), Dostoevsky recalls Sir Walter Scott's novel *The Monastery.*

14. I. I. Zamotin demonstrates the similarity between the plots of *Yury Miloslavsky* and Walter Scott's *A Legend of Montrose.* In the words of this scholar: "Zagoskin needed not a simple plot, but an interestingly structured and effect-filled one," which he found in many of the Scottish writer's novels. He was the first to apply the literary manner of Scott on Russian soil. But his possible attraction for Dostoevsky could be not only the external aspect of his writing, but his whole general trend. "The story of Russian spiritual truth and of foreign, particularly French, falsehood—that is the constant theme of his works," says Zamotin. "Zagoskin's romantic nationalism was close to the Slavophile worldview, and his novel is clear proof of the tie in idea and form between Russian Slavophilism and European romantic idealism." Zamotin, *Romanticism in Russian Literature in the Twenties,* I, 347, 377.